THE UNIVERSITY OF MICHIGAN
CENTER FOR JAPANESE STUDIES

MICHIGAN PAPERS IN JAPANESE STUDIES
NO. 2

PARTIES, CANDIDATES, AND VOTERS IN JAPAN:
SIX QUANTITATIVE STUDIES

Edited by

John Creighton Campbell

Ann Arbor

Center for Japanese Studies
The University of Michigan

1981

Copyright © 1981

by

Center for Japanese Studies
The University of Michigan

Library of Congress Cataloging in Publication Data

Main entry under title:

Parties, candidates, and voters in Japan.

(Michigan papers in Japanese studies; no. 2)

1. Political parties—Japan—Addresses, essays, lectures. 2. Elections—Japan—Addresses, essays, lectures. I. Campbell, John Creighton. II. Series.
JQ1698.A1P37   324'.0952   81-6190
ISBN 0-939512-07-6   AACR2

Printed in the United States of America

TABLE OF CONTENTS

Preface
    John Creighton Campbell   vii

Electoral Systems and the Basis of the Vote:
The Case of Japan
    Thomas R. Rochon   1

Social Environmental Effects upon Party Attachments:
The Cases of Italy and Japan
    John Strate   29

Political Participation and Policy Preference
in Japan
    Soo Young Auh   83

Candidates and Party Images: Recruitment to the
Japanese House of Representatives, 1958 - 1972
    Jung-Suk Youn   101

The Perceptions and Attitudes of Japanese
Candidates Toward Electoral Factors
    Minoru Yanagihashi   117

Gubernatorial Elections in Japan
    Steven R. Reed   139

Notes on Contributors   169

Preface

The study of voting and behavior associated with voting is the most developed subfield of American political science, in terms of both theoretical elaboration and empirical research. It is quite amenable to cross-national comparison, as much excellent research in Europe indicates. Voting research has also been popular among specialists on Japanese politics. Japan shares its level of economic development and many institutional structures with Western countries, but the cultural setting—presumably including political culture—is distinctive. It thus offers a splendid testing ground for broadening culture-bound theories of political behavior, as well as providing some fascinating puzzles of its own.

The essays collected in this volume deal with several theories and several puzzles. John Strate draws ingeniously on Japanese (and Italian) survey data to construct a fundamental critique of the concept of party identification, that most basic component of American-style research on the voting decision. His paper suggests a new linkage between social change and shifts in party support. Soo Young Auh deals with political participation, another well explored body of theory, but he treats levels of participation as an independent variable which helps explain variations in opinions on issues (including the security treaty and constitutional revision) among party adherents. Tom Rochon's crisp paper finally answers the old question of why Japanese tend to vote "for the man" rather than on the basis of party or issue orientation: it is not the personalistic culture, it is the electoral system. All three authors have relied mainly on secondary analysis of the large election survey carried out in 1967 by Robert E. Ward and Akira Kubota.

The other three papers focus on candidates and elections. Jung-Suk Youn has collected an impressive amount of data on those who ran for the Lower House of the Diet in the postwar period. His analysis of recruitment patterns emphasizes differences between parties and over time. Minoru Yanagihashi conducted his own survey of local and national candidates in Hyogo Prefecture to see how their perceptions of the importance of various electoral factors vary by party and level. His study throws new light on the role of the <u>yūryokusha,</u> the "men of influence" often seen as dominating election campaigns. Finally, Steven Reed has looked closely at aggregate election data along with case-study evidence to assess the importance of the "incumbency effect," the "second-term barrier" and the progressive local government movement on who comes to power in Japanese prefectures.

All these research projects were begun while the authors were graduate students in the Department of Political Science here at Michigan. The contributions by Auh, Yanagihashi and Youn were drawn from their Ph.D. dissertations, all initiated when Robert Ward was teaching Japanese politics. Rochon and Strate are not Japan specialists, but they courageously took on these topics in a research seminar I directed. Reed's essay was written especially for this volume. These younger scholars are now scattered quite widely--two in Korea, one each in Massachusetts, New Jersey, Alabama and Arizona—and it is very satisfying for me to be able to gather their important and interesting research on Japanese elections into this collection.

John Creighton Campbell

ELECTORAL SYSTEMS AND THE BASIS OF THE VOTE:
THE CASE OF JAPAN

Thomas R. Rochon

The question of how citizens make up their minds how to vote is an important and long-debated issue among behaviorists in political science. Conceptually, nearly all parties to the discussion follow the formulation of <u>The American Voter</u> (Campbell, Converse, Miller, and Stokes 1960), in which electoral variance is carved up into a long-term component, consisting of party identification, and a short-term component, consisting of individual evaluations of issues and candidates. Thus the vote can be seen as a decision representing the summation of forces on the voter. Viewed in this straightforward manner, the question becomes how the voter will weight each of the three forces (party identification, evaluation of issues, and evaluation of candidates). Will any two overcome a noncongruent third force? Or will one overpower the other two under certain circumstances?

In the United States, the evidence is sufficiently ambiguous to allow sharp disagreement as to the weighting of each of these three elements of electoral decision. This disagreement, which centers particularly on the relative importance of party and issues, may be discouraging to would-be cross-national researchers because the situation becomes even more complex when one must take into account variation in party systems and electoral systems. In this study I intend to compare the importance of the different components of the vote cross-nationally and, by looking at the case of Japan, argue that systemic variations may account for many of the cross-national differences in the weighting of these three components of electoral decision. However, it is important to note first the way in which the controversy that has plagued American studies is avoided here.

That controversy appears to have two sources. The first involves the simple question of change over time. There was, in the 1960s, a parallel decline in the strength of party attachments and a rise in the structuring of mass attitudes into ideologies in the United States (Nie and Anderson 1974; Converse and Markus 1979). As a consequence, the issue component of the voting decision has risen relative to the party component. Much of the disagreement has resulted from a focus on different elections, and to uncertainties about the impact of question wording on the degree of structuring of attitudes (Bishop, Tuchfarber, and Oldendick 1978; Sullivan, Piereson, and Marcus 1978). In sum, arguments about the relative importance of parties and issues depend in part on which era one is talking about.

The second, more intractable, source of difference is grounded in the artificial realm of methodology. The three components of the vote are obviously not entirely independent of each other because of selective learning and psychological distortion. In particular, party identification, to the extent that it is an ingrained attitude, will act as a filter on both the selection and evaluation of information related to candidates and issues. At the same time, persistently biased perceptions of issues can lead to a change in candidate evaluation and in party identification.[1] The three determinants of the vote—party, candidates, and issue attitudes—are also _mutually_ determining. This means that much of the variance in the vote must actually be attributed to several of the components jointly, and that any attempt to divide all the variance of the vote into three mutually exclusive sectors is arbitrary.

There are ways to avoid both of these areas of controversy, though in each case with some weakening of the power of the results. Since the present investigation is cross-sectional, the problem of change over time is simply ignored. One can control statistically for some sources of change over time, such as increasing education. Others, such as "the nature of the times," cannot be controlled for. Thus, some of the cross-national variation to be observed may stem from the fact that at the time of the survey one country was in a quiescent period like that of the American fifties, while another was in an issue-oriented political turmoil like the United States during the late 1960s. Such factors are not considered here, although Japanese voters will be shown to be relatively unconcerned with issues at the time of the 1967 election.

---

1. An example of selective perception leading to distortion of candidates' stances on the issues can be found in King 1977. Although candidate attachment may affect issue perceptions, no candidate has appeared on the American scene who by himself was able to permanently change partisan identifications (at least, not since the advent of public opinion research).

The second problem, that of the partition of common variance, is dealt with here by having individuals name the main reason why they voted as they did. This question is asked in most election studies in an open-ended form that allows the respondent to give any information at all that he or she considers important in reaching a voting decision. This tells us, for each voter, the single most important reason behind his choice, but does not permit any within-individual ranking of the three general forces posited in the standard psychological model. This is something of a weakness in analytic terms, yet that very weakness allows us to avoid the partitioning-of-variance controversy. Rather than evaluating the strength of forces within each individual, we can aggregate the single most important reason for the vote for the electorates in each of the countries studied.

This aggregation has been done in Table 1. The table shows that there is a considerable amount of variation between countries on the basis of the vote. It is the thesis of this paper that most of this variation is attributable not so much to cultural predispositions of the electorates of these countries as to electoral system differences. Japan will be analyzed to show that, contrary to the speculations of most of the literature, electoral arrangements do affect the choice of cues used in deciding how to vote.

TABLE 1
A Cross-National Comparison of the
Main Basis of the Vote

Country	Vote Based Upon			Weighted
	Party	Candidate	Issues	N
West Germany (1965)	59.6%	23.8%	16.6%	857
Netherlands (1967)	54.2	3.2	42.6	1478
Canada (1965)	48.4	32.5	19.1	1593
Japan (1967)	25.4	60.4	14.3	801
Great Britain (1966)	24.9	5.4	69.3	1500
United States (1968)	21.6	43.3	35.1	1851

Note: All datasets are from the archives of the Inter-University Consortium for Political and Social Research. The American study is from the 1968 presidential election. The basis of the vote question is not asked in connection with the congressional elections. Dutch data are unweighted.

Before turning to Japan, it would be worthwhile to look briefly at the basis of the vote in some of the other countries to check its plausibility in terms of their electoral systems. Looking first at the candidate column in

Table 1, it is not surprising that voters in Great Britain and the Netherlands put very little stress on the candidate. With a party list system and a single, nation-wide electoral district, for instance, the Dutch find "candidate" a particularly meaningless cue. Even the 5 and 3 percent responses recorded in these countries represent references to the party leader rather than to local candidates. The same is true of the one-quarter of respondents who voted on the basis of the candidate in Germany. Candidate emphasis there results from the visibility of the party leaders in the "Chancellor's democracy," rather than from the German electoral system (in which voters cast two ballots, one for a party and one for a candidate). The same stress on the candidate is, of course, even more prevalent in American presidential elections, a fact which is neatly borne out by the figures in Table 1.

The Japanese and Canadian candidate responses differ from those of the other countries in that they refer to the <u>local</u> candidate. These two cases show that a parliamentary democracy need not be totally party-oriented, as is sometimes inferred from the British case alone. The great stress on candidates in Japan will be the subject of further analysis at a later point.

Given the above comments on the Dutch electoral system, it is not surprising that Dutch voters place great emphasis on party in casting their votes. What is surprising is that it is Canada and not Great Britain that joins them in this respect. I am at a loss to explain the lack of a greater stress on party in Great Britain or, to look at the other side of the coin, their great stress on issues. In looking at the proportions of issue-oriented voters across nations, it is important to remember that the criteria for inclusion in the issues column were very lax (see the Appendix for details of the coding process). This column no doubt benefitted most from the partition of the overlap between vote bases. The issue column also has the most variance, as might be expected since at any given moment the emphasis on issues probably has more to do with a particular election campaign than with a country's electoral system. The 1967 election in the Netherlands, for example, was the first in a series of elections in which the old party system was successfully challenged by new-party insurgents whose platforms contradicted some of the traditional operations of Dutch politics. Previous elections there were decided much more on the basis of partisanship. A survey taken in 1956 in the Netherlands, for example, found that 70 percent said they voted on the basis of party, and only 30 percent on the basis of issues (<u>De Nederlandse Kiezer</u> 1956).

The Basis of the Vote in Japan

The rest of this study is devoted to Japan, and the first subject of attention is the fact that the Japanese are the least likely to mention issues as the most important factor in their voting choices. It is worth noting that Japan is very near the six-nation median with respect to party (see Table 1), although it would be more accurate to say that it belongs to the cluster of three countries that gives party more emphasis.

The heavy stress upon the candidate among voters will surprise Japanese scholars not at all. It has often been noted that candidates for Japan's Diet stress <u>themselves</u> in their campaigns: their virtue, the fact that they are from the local area, and so on. An in-depth study of how one candidate organized his campaign for the Diet showed that party identification was considered to mark the boundary of potential support, but was not appealed to <u>per se</u> (Curtis 1971). The question, then, is why the voters respond to the personalistic appeals of the candidates. Here the dominant argument is that various elements of the Japanese culture cause politics to be conducted on a person-to-person level. Bradley Richardson has stated this cultural argument particularly well:[2]

> The ongoing networks of personal influence and interpersonal connections that form the backbone of Japanese community life are extensively cultivated by individual candidates in order to build up support . . . It is quite clear that many voters stress candidate character in their choices simply on the assumption that public officials should have exemplary personal qualities. Preferences for candidates of high moral caliber also include concern for the election of representatives whose quality and behavior will favorably reflect upon the constituencies supporting them . . . Japanese typically depend on personal benefactors to a degree uncommon in most Western societies; they prefer to work through known intermediaries in many kinds of situations rather than deal with persons who are unknown. (1974:114-16)

---

2. More generally on the same topic, see Richardson (1974), Chapters 5 and 6. A similar point about personalism in Japanese society as a whole is a major theme in sociological studies. See Ishida (1971), Chapters 6 and 7, and Nakane (1970), Chapter 2. The theme of "patron-client democracy" pervades the text of Ike (1972). Richardson elsewhere recognizes the importance of the electoral system in causing the stress on candidates (Flanagan and Richardson 1977:40).

Some notion of the flavor of this cultural trait of personalism is given in some of the "untranslatable" words that frequently appear in descriptions of Japanese politics. For example, there are the _jiban_, or bailiwicks. _Jiban_, in the candidates' home districts, are characterized by _jimoto_ (localism) and _suisensei_ (the process by which the village elders form a consensus and then recommend their chosen candidate to the whole village). The recommendation system can be so effective that it results in a village bloc vote, allowing candidates to calculate very closely how many and which village recommendations they must get in order to win a seat. Lastly, there are the _kōenkai_, or support groups, that function rather like social clubs but which revolve around prospective Dietmen. _Suisensei_ and _kōenkai_ are both workable because of the prevalence of _giri_, or personal obligation, and the many examples of _oyabun-Kobun_, or "father-son" (patron-client) relationships.[3]

Of course, it may be argued that all cultures have the elements of what we might call the personalistic tradition. Admiration for the moral man, attachment to the "favorite son," susceptibility to face-to-face appeals, reliance on the recommendations of local elites (be they village elders or urban newspaper editors), and candidate-centered organizations that exist independently of party groups are all commonly found in other democracies. The question is whether they are more frequent or more important in Japan, enough so to account for the fact that many more voters in Japan than elsewhere give first priority to the candidate in casting their ballots.

There is an alternative explanation to the question of why the Japanese are so candidate-oriented in their voting choices. The second explanation is that the unusual electoral system which the Japanese use often forces voters to base their final decision on the candidate himself. The unique aspect of the Japanese electoral system is that it often presents the voters with the choice of more than one candidate running in his or her party. The voter must cast a ballot for a given individual, not for a party list. However, because Japan employs multi-member districts, with the seats going to the top finishers in the district, the larger Japanese parties often nominate more than one candidate per district.[4] The result is that once a voter has decided which

---

3. _Kōenkai, jiban_, etc., are described vividly in Reischauer (1978), Chapter 27.
4. In practice, only two parties—the Liberal Democratic Party (LDP) and the Japan Socialist Party (JSP)—are ever confident of enough support in a district that they are willing to nominate more than one candidate in a single district. For the other parties, nominating two or more people would just fragment the party's support so that neither candidate could get enough votes

party to vote for, the electoral decision is still left unsettled, for the voter must still decide which of the party's several nominees to support.

That choice can only be made on the basis of the candidates themselves.[5] This situation also explains why candidates for the Diet are forced to emphasize their moral qualities, their local roots, etc., so heavily in their campaigns. When a candidate finds himself competing for votes not only with candidates from other parties, but also with other candidates from his own party, a purely partisan appeal obviously will not be enough to ensure a victory.

It is possible to disentangle these two rival explanations of why the Japanese voter is so candidate-oriented in order to see how important each is in explaining the phenomenon. If it is Japan's traditional culture which is most important in causing the candidate-orientation of most Japanese voters, then the candidate-orientation should be most prevalent among those who are most clearly tied to the values of that traditional culture. If, on the other hand, it is the plurality of choices within the party which accounts for the high level of candidate-oriented voting in Japan, then we should see this candidate-orientation primarily in districts where there were two or more nominees from the party which the voter intends to support. In situations where the voter's party has only one nominee there will still be some people who vote on the basis of candidate, but unless the cultural factor is also operating, that figure should be no higher than it is for other countries listed in Table 1.

to be elected. Since a party cannot pool the votes of its candidates after the election to produce one winner from several losers, careful calculation of expected electoral support for the party in each district is a must for party leaders.

5. Since each of the multiple nominations tends to be made by a different faction within the LDP or JSP, it would be possible for a voter to make a choice among several party nominees through identification with a faction rather than through the candidate. This possibility can be disposed of rather easily: <u>not one</u> respondent in the 1967 Ward-Kubota study mentioned factions when asked the main reason they voted as they did. Thus, although 36 percent of the respondents knew that the LDP is split into factions, and 34 percent were aware that the JSP is split into factions, that awareness has no resonance in voting behavior in Japan. Nor are those who are aware of the presence of factions in those two parties more likely to vote on the basis of candidate when the number of candidates running in the district with LDP or JSP endorsement is controlled for.

TABLE 2
Main Basis of the Vote in Japan
by Number of Party Nominees in Voters' Districts

Basis of Vote	Number of Party Nominees				
	One	Two	Three	Four	Five
Party	49.8%	30.7%	10.3%	8.2%	0.0%
Candidate	36.3	52.4	76.4	82.4	88.9
Issues	13.8	16.9	13.3	9.4	11.1
Total	99.9%	100.0%	100.0%	100.0%	100.0%
Weighted N	160	302	195	85	18

Table 2 provides striking confirmation that the electoral system does indeed cause the Japanese to emphasize the candidate when they cast their votes. Of those who voted for a party with one nominee in their district, only 36 percent voted on the basis of candidate, a proportion smaller than that of candidate-voters in the United States and only slightly larger than the proportion in Canada. The jump between 36 percent in the case of one party nominee and 52 percent in the case of two party nominees is large and important: in terms of deciding how to vote, party preference can completely determine the choice when there is one candidate, but not when there are two or more from the same party. This 16 percentage point gap between the one-candidate and the two-candidate situations is smaller than the difference between the cases of two party nominees and three. While it is obvious why candidate-based voting occurs more frequently in districts with two party nominees than in districts with only one, it is less obvious why the percentage voting on the basis of candidate should continue to increase as even more nominees are added. Perhaps the greater density of candidate-based claims and counter-claims in the multi-candidate situation adds to the personalistic atmosphere of the campaign as a whole, thus inducing more people to vote on the basis of candidate traits.

The differences between the one- and two-candidate cases and the two- and three-candidate cases, in terms of increasing emphasis on the candidate and decreasing emphasis on the party, are each on the order of a 20 percent shift. The differences between the three-candidates case and the more-than-three candidates cases are much more modest, which is in line with our expectations. Also of interest is the relatively constant proportion of voters in all kinds of districts choosing on the basis of issues. Discrimination of candidates' issue positions is logically sufficient to arrive at a voting choice no matter how many candidates there are. Hence issue-oriented voting should not vary by the number of candidates being offered by the voter's party. It is the widespread lack of political information and interest, rather than the electoral system, that keeps this figure so small.[6]

One possible explanation for the pattern in Table 2 is that it is really a reflection of differences between the supporters of different parties. The parties are not evenly distributed across the table. As noted, only the LDP and the JSP ever nominate more than one individual in a district. In fact, the columns with four and five party nominees are composed entirely of LDP voters,[7] while the column with three party nominees is 80 percent LDP. The two-candidate column, on the other hand, is only one-third LDP and two-thirds JSP. The column with one party nominee is composed mostly of the smaller parties, the Clean Government Party (CGP), Democratic Socialist Party (DSP) and Japan Communist Party (JCP), but also has about one-third JSP voters. Virtually all LDP voters are presented with at least two nominees from their party.

Does the relationship in Table 2 between number of candidates and the basis of the vote result solely from the differing partisan composition of the different categories? Table 3 presents the same relationship once again, this time controlling for party. It is only possible to analyze the JSP and the LDP, of course, since they are the only two parties with any variation in number of candidates nominated per district. Whether supporters of the smaller parties would behave differently if faced with more than one nominee from their party is a moot point.

Table 3 shows the same pattern of continuing steps that Table 2 does, but to a lesser degree. Indeed, the reason that the step between two and three candidates was larger than the step between one candidate and two in Table 2 is that LDP supporters on the whole are more likely than JSP

---

6. This is not to imply that Japanese levels of political information and political interest are lower than levels typical of Western Europe and the United States. They are not.
7. Only two sampled districts had five candidates, the LDP strongholds of Ibaraki 3 and Mie 1. Eighteen respondents of these two districts reported voting for the LDP, and of these, sixteen, or 89%, reported voting mainly on the basis of candidate. The four respondents in Table 3 who voted for the only LDP candidate available to them were all from the 6th election district of Tokyo. Although a N of 4 carries no statistical weight at all, this column is kept separate in order to keep the two-candidate category pure, since the most crucial distinction in number of candidates is precisely between one and more than one.

supporters to vote on the basis of candidate. Part of the explanation for this is that LDP voters are usually faced with more party nominees than are JSP voters. But it is also clear, for reasons to be investigated later, that LDP voters are simply more likely to vote on the basis of candidate. For example, when faced with two nominees, 47 percent of JSP voters chose on the basis of candidate, while 64 percent of LDP voters in the same situation did so. The same comparison can be made between JSP and LDP voters faced with a choice between among three party nominees. The primary lesson from looking at the parties separately, however, is that the difference between voters faced with different numbers of nominees is not due solely to their different party attachments. Also, while adding more nominees always makes a voter more likely to choose on the basis of candidate, the most important difference is between voters faced with one party nominee and voters having to choose between more than one nominee from the same party.

TABLE 3
Basis of the Vote by Number of Candidates,
Party Controlled

A. All JSP Voters

Basis of Vote	Candidates		
	One	Two	Three
Party	57.1%	35.5%	21.7%
Candidate	25.5	46.9	60.9
Issues	17.4	17.6	17.4
Total	100.0%	100.0%	100.0%
Weighted N	58	205	230

B. All LDP Voters

Basis of Vote	Candidates				
	One	Two	Three	Four	Five
Party	83.7%	20.6%	8.7%	8.2%	0.0%
Candidate	16.3	64.0	78.5	82.4	88.9
Issues	0.0	15.4	12.8	9.4	11.1
Total	100.0%	100.0%	100.0%	100.0%	100.0%
Weighted N	4	97	172	85	18

Incidentally, the data presented here help explain the finding that party identification, while widespread in Japan, is not held with much intensity (Richardson 1974:118-23; Kubota, n.d.).[8] Party identification is generally acquired from early socialization experiences in the family—hence the great predictive power of parents' party identification—and is reinforced or changed throughout the life cycle in response to adult socialization forces (for example at work), and in response to political events. One of the reinforcers which helps create the usual pattern of party identification, in which its strength increases with age, is the repetition of the experience of watching the party's candidates perform during the political campaign. This is a time of peak political attention for most people, and voting for the party nominee on election day renews and strengthens attachment to the party.[9] That relationship does not hold in Japan: the strength of party identification increases very little throughout the life cycle.

As we have seen, most voters in Japan are exposed to campaigns in which candidates are forced to run against, and hence criticize, other nominees of their own party. On top of that, since party is not usually a sufficient basis on which to make a choice, the voter is unable to feel the satisfaction of having voted for the party; a voter chooses one of several contending party nominees and hence has voted in the party, but not for the party. Thus, while the early socialization mechanisms may well be doing their job in planting the seed of a partisan identification,[10] an important source of continuing reinforcement is missing. The logical result is widespread but weakly-held partisan attachment, which is the pattern that in fact occurs.

It should be emphasized that this explanation of the extent and depth of party identification is just speculation. It does fit the facts as far as the efficacy of socialization, the campaign style of the candidates, and the widely but shallowly held party identification patterns go. However, the link between the number of candidates and the strength of party identification,

---

8. Richardson presents good cross-national data on the subject; see Table 1 of Richardson (1975).
9. The best explication of this process is to be found in Converse (1976).
10. Robert Ward and Akira Kubota (1970) find that the family does in fact operate effectively as a socializer of party attachments in Japan. Party identification is more clearly passed from parent to child than are either issue positions or level of political interest. The Tau-b measuring congruence of party affiliation between parent and child in Japan is .39; this is nearly as high as in the United States where Tau-b is .47. Ward and Kubota conclude that the lower strength of party identification in Japan cannot be attributed to socialization effects.

unlike the link between the number of candidates and the basis of the vote, cannot be demonstrated. For the LDP, the strength of party identification is higher in districts with few LDP candidates than in districts with many, but the difference is not statistically significant and may simply be an artifact of other differences between those constituencies.[11] For the JSP, the average strength of party identification is actually higher in districts with more than one candidate, contrary to our expectations.

Thus, the number of candidates of a voter's party in the district predicts the basis of the voter's choice, but not the strength of his partisan attachment. This is part of a broader pattern in which the number of party candidates predicts attitudes that are immediate and instrumental to the election, but not attitudes that may be considered more deeply held, transcending any particular election. In other words, the number of candidates from his own party that a voter is faced with is seen as part of the context of the immediate political campaign. It is a fact relevant only for temporary attitudes and behaviors that are directly related to that campaign.

An example of a temporary attitude, which serves as an instrumental piece of information for the duration of the campaign only, is whether the voter can remember the name of the candidate voted for a few weeks after the election (see Figure 1). The pattern of candidate remembrance for the LDP voters is intuitively sensible: where only one LDP candidate was offered in the district, relatively few people who voted for him could recall his name later. After all, they did not need to pay a great deal of attention to the candidate himself (Table 3 tells us that they voted on the basis of party). Where there are two candidates, of course, the situation immediately changes and recall of the candidate's name rises dramatically. Finally, where more than two candidates are available, some confusion sets in and the proportion of voters who can recall the name of the candidate they voted for again declines (slightly).

This relationship is not as clear-cut for JSP voters. First, the pattern of declining memory in multiple-candidacy situations does not hold. Nor does the proportion recalling their candidate's name vary much between the one-

---

11. On the other hand, the LDP easily has the lowest overall strength of partisan attachment among its supporters. The usual explanation is the LDP's lack of strong local party organizations; but that may also be an effect of multiple candidacies. In other words, one reason why the LDP is organizationally weak at the grass-roots level may be precisely because it is large enough to field several candidates in each district.

nominee and the two-nominee cases. While the differences that do exist go in the right direction, they are not statistically significant. Since, for the LDP, the decline in candidate remembrance really begins only when there are more than three candidates, it is possible that the JSP simply never offers enough candidates to confuse its voters very much.

To summarize, the number of candidates offered by a party in a district affects the basis on which the vote is cast and the ability to remember the name of the individual for whom one voted. Both of these questions tap fairly transitory phenomena that are closely related to the election itself and would not be picked up in a survey of political attitudes that did not focus on a particular election. This does not mean that these things are unimportant: the basis of electoral choice is profoundly relevant for the way campaigns are conducted, the kind of people who are elected, and, presumably, the kinds of policies that are eventually pursued.

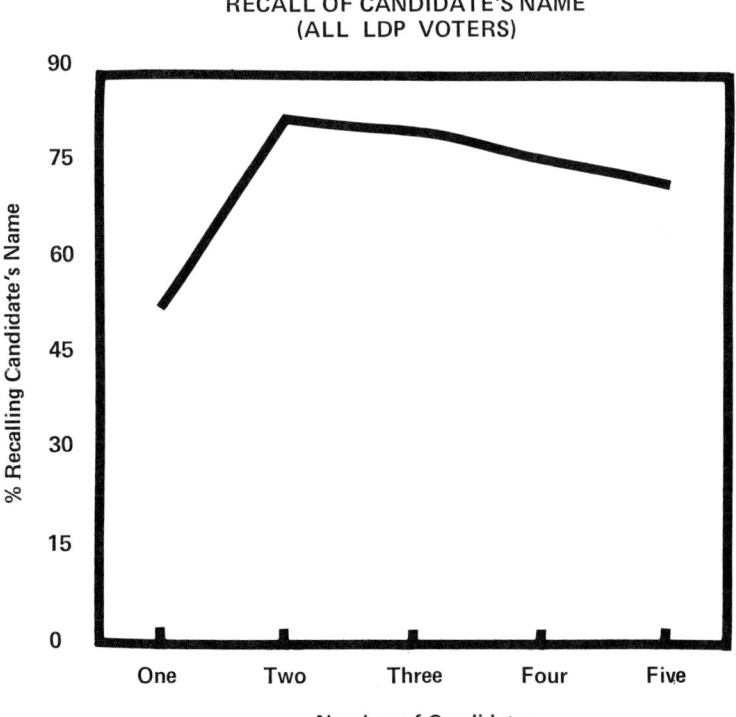

FIGURE 1: NUMBER OF PARTY NOMINEES AND RECALL OF CANDIDATE'S NAME (ALL LDP VOTERS)

Still, we may ask whether the number of candidates offered by a party in a political district affects some of the more deeply or permanently held attitudes of Japanese voters. The answer is very clear: no. The number of candidates offered by one's party might plausibly be assumed to affect the likelihood of seeing government as too complex, of seeing important differences between the two parties, of being interested in the election campaign, and of being aware that the LDP and the JSP are each divided into factions. As it turns out, none of these things are affected by the number of candidates of one's own party--not efficacy, not interest, not even awareness of factions.[12] And, as already noted, the strength of party identification is not affected by the number of candidates. In short, the more fundamental political values are not affected by the number of candidates offered in a district by one's own party. Those attitudes are formed by other experiences, perhaps by experiences that are more clearly related to daily life and not related only to the election campaigns that take place once every few years.

A Rival Explanation: Japan's Political Culture

The evidence presented so far strongly supports the theory that the unique properties of Japan's electoral system, rather than any cultural factors, cause Japanese voters to cast their ballots on the basis of candidate appeal. But the successful test of one explanation does not necessarily rule out the other. Are cultural factors lurking in the background, rendering the apparent relationship between the number of candidates nominated by a party and the basis of the vote spurious? Alternatively, could political culture and the electoral system both be pressing the Japanese voter to make a choice on the basis of candidate evaluations?

A test of the cultural hypothesis is clearly called for, and a measure of the urbanicity of each electoral district can provide that test.[13] Political culture is a matter of political attitudes, and, of course, an urban/rural variable does not directly measure these at all. In Japan, however, urban and rural areas are light years apart in terms of precisely these cultural

---

12. Data not presented. The finding that awareness of factions is not connected to the basis of the vote is the most surprising of these results, since nominees in multi-candidate districts are chosen on a factional basis.
13. I am grateful to Jung-Suk Youn for providing the Densely Inhabited District Index for each of the electoral districts in Japan. The figures come from the 1970 census, the census closest to the 1967 survey. Further details on the meaning of the DID Index may be found in Table 4.

variables. Richardson (1974) summarizes the differences succinctly: rural voters emphasize personalities in politics, while party labels are seen as less important.[14]

In addition, rural areas in Japan have some of the same characteristics associated with rural areas in all industrialized nations: less education, less intensive exposure to the mass media, and so on. The fact that the LDP is strongest in the countryside, and thus runs more candidates there, while the JSP is weaker in the countryside, and thus can be expected to run fewer candidates there, completes the circle; one could infer from these facts that the observed relationship between number of candidates and the basis of the vote is at least potentially spurious.

The evidence suggests that the cultural factor is operating alongside, or independent of, the influence of the electoral system. Table 4 shows that there is a strong relationship in the expected direction between urban/rural status and voting on the basis of candidate or party. In every party, especially in the two larger ones, those who voted on the basis of candidate come from more rural areas than those who voted by party. Table 4 also shows that those who voted on the basis of issues are as rural, or more so, as those who voted by candidate. This occurs despite the fact that candidate voting is generally assumed to be associated with a traditional outlook and thus to be found more often in rural areas.

This suggests that it is possible to vote on the basis of candidate whether one is modern or traditional. Two observers of the Japanese electorate point out that "the most traditional form of voting behavior in Japan is the ratification of authority" (Scalapino and Masumi 1962), i.e., voting on the basis of the recommendation of an accepted authority figure. According to this view, as the Japanese have become more modern in their attitudes, they are more likely to make individual voting decisions. Their decisions may still be based primarily on the candidate, but will be made independently of the traditional authorities in the family and community.

---

14. Richardson (1974) performs a multivariate analysis and discovers that the greater part of urban-rural differences is washed out when education is controlled. The same result was found in this study (see Table 8). This finding does not affect the present analysis. Our concern is with political culture or patterns of political attitudes, and the fact that there is considerable urban-rural variance in those attitudes justifies pitting the urban/rural variable against number of candidates as a predictor of the basis of the vote, no matter what the original source of the urban-rural difference is.

TABLE 4
Basis of the Vote by DID Index

	Mean DID Score		
Basis of Vote	LDP Voters	JSP Voters	Other Voters
Party	56.7	54.7	72.3
Candidate	42.2	47.8	69.1
Issues	46.2	45.0	65.5
Weighted N	350	258	96
Eta	.19	.13	.06

Note: The Densely Inhabited District (DID) Index is the official census definition of urbanicity in Japan. It is the proportion of the people in the respondent's district who are living in an area with more than 75,000 people per square kilometer. As a percentage, it can vary from 0 (the most rural areas) to 100 (the most urban areas).

This distinction perhaps explains the different patterns of ruralness and basis of the vote that exist in the different parties. For the LDP, issue voters are in between the other two groups of voters in degree of ruralness. Issue voters are the most rural group in their party only outside of the LDP. This makes sense when one considers that community party cues in rural areas are not likely to support any but the LDP. Apparently, if one is going to be a socialist in a rural area, one is likely to arrive at that position by referring to the issues and not to the locally dominant party symbols. Furthermore, to remain a socialist (or anything but a Liberal Democrat) in the face of a hostile local environment, it is likely that an individual will continually need to refer to the issues in order to defend his position.

In short, the relationship observed in Table 4 between urban/rural status and the basis of the vote holds strongly only for the LDP. The reasons that rural JSP voters do not act like "rurals" in terms of the basis of the vote are two:

1) They live in a conservative environment in which maintaining a loyalty to the JSP requires a positive commitment to that party and to its stance on the issues.

2) They need not vote on the basis of the candidate because the JSP rarely puts up more than one candidate for election in a rural district.

We can go a step further by examining the relationship between urban/rural status and basis of the vote in the LDP with the number of candidates controlled for. If the major explanation for high candidate-oriented voting is really that rural voters are predisposed to vote on the basis of candidate, then it should make no difference how many candidates they are offered. Table 5 presents the urbanicity scores for LDP voters faced with different numbers of candidates as well as those who had no choice of candidates within their own party.

Within each category of number of candidates offered, the original relationship between urban/rural status and basis of the vote is sharply attenuated. While urban/rural status maintains some statistical relationship with the basis of the vote, and a pretty good one in the three-candidate case for the LDP, its effects are pale next to the structural features of multiple candidacies within the parties. Note also that in the case of the LDP voters with two party candidates to choose from, the party-based voters are actually more rural than the candidate-based voters. Finally, the urbanicity index cannot account for differences in the basis of the vote among those who have only one candidate to choose from. This illustrates the general conclusion that while urban/rural status does partially account for party vs. candidate voting, it adds very little predictive power to the number-of-candidates explanation.

TABLE 5
DID Index and Basis of the Vote,
Number of Candidates Controlled

Basis of Vote	LDP Voters Number of Candidates			All Voters One Candidate
	Two	Three	Four/Five	
Party	67.1	39.1	40.8	64.6
Candidate	70.6	31.4	37.5	65.4
Issues	70.9	32.0	36.2	61.5
Weighted N	92	159	94	150
Eta	.03	.13	.05	.01

A slightly different approach to the analysis of the effects of political culture on the basis of voting choice would be to separate people into traditional and modern categories on the basis of their answers to social attitude questions. In a sense, this approach is preferable to the urban/rural split because it does not assume that all the modern people are found in the cities and all the traditional people in the countryside. If, for example, the psychology of the rural JSP voter really is different from the more typical rural conservative, then he has a good chance of being separated from them on a social attitude item.

The 1967 Ward-Kubota study of the Japanese electorate included a battery of questions that are directed at uncovering modern or traditional aspects of the respondent's thinking. There are twelve questions organized around three major topics. First, there is a series of four questions about the emperor: whether there should be one, what his powers and political role should be, and whether he should live differently from other people. Next, there are three questions tapping the importance of community and harmony to the respondent: whether he would protest unfair treatment at the hands of a government official, whether he would object to a community decision, and whether he would donate to a charity that he didn't like. Third, a series of five questions tapped miscellaneous social attitudes: toward the role of women and young people, toward the importance of discipline and frugality, and toward the relative weight of individual and family considerations in the making of decisions.

TABLE 6
Modernity and the Basis of the Vote

Basis of Vote	Emperor Factor	Mean Score Community Factor	Social Factor
Party	3.03	2.94	2.31
Candidate	2.62	2.42	2.13
Issues	2.77	2.46	2.08
Weighted N	756	728	786
Eta	.16	.14	.09

Note: Each factor is an additive index of the number of "modern" responses given to each series of questions as described in the text. The range of scores for each factor is from 1 (most traditional) to 5 (most modern).

A factor analysis was performed on these items to see whether they cluster on a single dimension that might be presumed to measure traditional or modern value structures (see the Appendix). Three factors emerged, however, as each series of questions was found to cohere, tapping different elements of what we usually think of as a single dimension of psychological modernity. In addition, one survey item which asks directly whether the respondent thinks of himself as a "new type of person" or an "old type of person" was found to correlate with all three dimensions, yet not be a complete part of any of them. This last measure, then, appears to behave as the survey designers intended it to. It summarizes the degree of tradition or modernity in the respondent's cultural attitudes.

We can now proceed to analyze the differences between candidate, party, and issue oriented voters in terms of their cultural attitudes. Table 6 presents the mean scores on the three modernity factors by basis of the vote for all respondents. A larger mean score indicates a more "modern" series of responses to the items in each factor. Two things are apparent in this table. First, voters who choose on the basis of candidates turn out to be more traditional on all three factors than voters who use party. Those who voted on the basis of issues are generally somewhere in between, continuing to confound the expectation that issue-based voting is the most enlightened and "modern" possible basis of the vote.[15] The second thing to emerge from Table 6 is that all three dimensions of modernity are not equal in their power to discriminate between types of voters. This is revealed by the size of the etas. Instead, the three factors are ordered in a very common-sense way: the Emperor factor taps a dimension which is very directly political, while the Community factor is slightly less so (it does, however, deal with community decision-making and relationships between citizens and government officials). The Social factor, in asking about the ideal relations in the family, between young and old, and between men and women, is perhaps closest to what we think of in terms of modernity and tradition, but the relatively tenuous link between social values and political behavior is made clear by the eta of .09.

Knowing that the degree of modernity has an effect, albeit a modest one, on the basis of the vote, tells us only part of what we want to know.

---

15. This result may occur in part because of the permissiveness of the "issues" category. Even the vaguest reference to issue or to group interest was coded as an issue response (see Appendix). However, it is also true that some issues, e.g., school issues, have greater salience in rural Japan than in the cities.

Table 7 contains scores on the Emperor factor, the most political of the three modernity dimensions, for the three types of voters, with party and number of candidates in the district controlled. The first (rather reassuring) finding is that JSP voters are consistently more modern than LDP voters. Of more direct interest here, though, is a comparison within parties of those who voted on the basis of candidate, party, or issues. The etas seem to indicate a fairly healthy relationship. When there are three candidates available, whether of the LDP or the JSP, candidate voters are likely to be more modern than party voters. In other cases, the Emperor factor scores for candidate and party voters are virtually identical, and it is the traditionalism of the issue voters that inflates the eta.

In sum, the relationship between traditionalism and basis of the vote is not a consistent one. The hypothesis that greater traditionalism in the multi-candidate district produces candidate-based votes there is not sustained. In fact, LDP voters in four-or-five-candidate districts are slightly more modern than LDP voters in two-candidate districts, which is counterintuitive, while multi-candidate JSP districts contain JSP voters only very slightly more modern than the JSP voters to be found in single-candidate JSP districts.

TABLE 7
Modernity and the Basis of the Vote,
Party and Number of Candidates Controlled

Basis of Vote	LDP Voters Number of Candidates			JSP Voters Number of Candidates		
	Two	Three	Four/Five	One	Two	Three
Party	2.49	2.44	2.55	3.08	3.25	3.00
Candidate	2.53	2.46	2.49	2.82	2.86	3.10
Issues	2.14	2.53	2.59	2.44	3.13	2.33
Weighted N	93	162	96	58	192	21
Eta	.16	.12	.18	.21	.16	.33

Note: Modernity is measured in this table by the Emperor factor. As in Table 6, higher scores mean more modern attitudes.

Nor does an analysis of the question of whether the respondent thinks of himself as a new or old type of person clear up the matter. This item correlated with all three of the modern/traditional factors, leading to an interpretation of it as a summary index of the various dimensions of modernity. When the basis of the vote is predicted from this summary question, conclusions similar to those obtained from analysis of the Emperor factor emerge. That is, JSP voters tend to be more modern than LDP voters. But within parties and with the number of candidates controlled, party voters do not emerge as consistently more modern than those who voted primarily by candidate.

We should be clear about exactly what this means. There are differences between supporters of the two main parties in terms of modernity. But once you know whether an individual voted for the LDP or JSP, knowing whether he also has modern or traditional attitudes tells nothing more about which of the three elements of voting choice he was likely to consider most important in casting his ballot.

A number of competing explanations of the candidate orientation of the Japanese voter have been tested. It has been suggested that the number of candidates in the district is the explanation that statistically dominates the others. This conclusion can be systematized with a Multiple Classification Analysis (MCA), a summary of which is presented in Table 8. The MCA is akin to a regression equation, but uses nominal level variables as predictors. Betas are computed for each of the predictors: they reflect the association between each predictor and the dependent variable, controlling for each of the other predictors. The results clearly show that the situational determinant, the number of candidates offered, dominates the several measures of personal characteristics (education, modernity of attitudes vis-a-vis the emperor, and self-assessment of modernity or traditionalism of attitudes). The weakest predictor, the urban/rural index, is also a situational variable, but is used as a proxy for a number of personal characteristics. Its weakness suggests that education and the two measures of modernity capture fully the effect of personal traits. The conclusion that Japanese voters are responding to the voting situation as structured by the electoral system in use in Japan is inescapable: the multiple R of .39 from the MCA equation is only slightly larger than the .34 that represents the bivariate correlation between number of candidates and the basis of the vote.

TABLE 8
Multiple Classification Analysis
Predicting Basis of the Vote

Predictor	Beta
Number of Candidates	.34
Education	.12
Emperor Factor	.10
New/Old Type	.06
DID Index (Urbanicity)	.03

Multiple R = .39

Note: For the purposes of this table, the basis of the vote was made dichotomous by dropping those who voted primarily on issues. This makes the dependent variable a party/candidate dichotomy. Also, the Emperor factor and the DID Index of urbanicity were both collapsed into four groups in order to accommodate the requirements of the MCA.

Conclusions

What are we to make of the view that political culture is an important, or the important, reason why the Japanese tend to vote the candidate? The operationalizations of political culture used here do not fare well at all. The urban/rural cleavage accounts for some differences in the level of candidate voting among LDP voters, but those differences do not hold up and are not in a consistent direction when the number of candidates is controlled. Furthermore, to summarize quickly data that need not be displayed here, the relationship between the number of candidates and the basis of the vote does hold up under the sequential application of a wide range of controls. This relationship is maintained no matter which party the respondent votes for (see Table 3), what his levels of political interest or information are, whether he is a rural or an urban resident, whether he has attitudes that can be classed as modern or not, and whether he considers himself a "new type" of person or not. No matter what, the Japanese voter is likely to decide how to vote on the basis of candidate when the party he votes for offers more than one nominee in his district. When faced with only one nominee, the Japanese voter may still vote on the basis of candidate, but is no more likely to do so than voters of other nations.[16]

16. Or at least no more likely than voters in most other nations with single-member electoral districts.

Even so, one final caveat about the level of candidate voting and its relationship to the Japanese political culture is in order. Many writers have stressed the fact that the traditional elements of Japanese culture are predominantly rural and localistic in nature. It would be a fallacy to think of national politics in Japan as primarily traditional, but such tendencies are more pronounced at the local level in many areas of the country. This suggestion is supported by the fact that candidate-oriented voting is even more common in Japan at the local than at the national level (Flanagan 1968; Tsurutani 1977:223-24).

The cultural characteristics which impel Japanese voters to choose on the basis of candidate can be found to some degree in many countries. What seems to make Japan unique is rather the electoral system that pits candidates of the same party against each other. And that is precisely the variable that is most closely related to the basis of the vote.

Several conclusions, and suggestions for further research, emerge from this analysis. The most obvious result is that the realm of behaviors attributed to "political culture" is now a bit smaller than it was previously. As comparativists are fond of moralizing, political culture is often used as a residual variable, accounting for otherwise unexplained variance between nations (Teune and Ostrowski 1973; Przeworski and Teune 1970).[17] To be a true explanatory variable, however, the attitudes it supposedly measures must be shown to be consistently held in a population and, if possible, the agent or agents that foster those attitudes must be located. When several countries are looked at in comparative perspective, aspects of individual political systems often appear to be part of a more general pattern not confined to one country. In this case, the fact that Japanese vote on the basis of candidate is incontrovertible. However, this is not a manifestation of their culture, but a response to the demands of their unique electoral system. Thus, if the electoral system were changed, voting on the basis of candidate in national elections should recede overnight to about one-third of the population, a level similar to candidate-based voting in other nations.

It remains to be discovered why the remaining one-third votes on the basis of candidate, or why _anyone_ votes for the reasons they do. But this research can now proceed on the assumption that, whatever the cause of the selection of the basis of the vote, Japanese voters are motivated by the same considerations as voters elsewhere.

---

17. This paper follows the strategy recommended by Teune and Ostrowski in that Japan is seen to fit cross-national patterns of basis of the vote through an analysis of the variance _within_ the country.

Although the Japanese electoral system is unique, the demands it places on voters in multi-candidate districts are not. In an American primary election, the same situation of having to choose among nominees of the same party occurs. The main finding of this paper seems sensible enough in this context: American primary voters can be expected to choose on the basis of candidate or issues, not party.

Yet the implications of that statement are rarely considered. First, those who are accustomed to voting on the basis of party may choose not to vote in the primary, leaving that election to those who generally vote the candidate (presumably the least politically involved portion of the population) and those who vote on the basis of issues (presumably the most politically involved portion of the population). More plausibly, people may vote on one basis in the primary and on another in the general election. The result could be that the candidate who does best in the primaries will not be the best vote-getter in the general election. We do know that divisive primaries in the United States have often led to defeat in the general election. This tends to hurt the locally dominant party (Bernstein 1977). The effect of the electoral system in Japan may thus have been to prevent the two largest parties, the LDP and the JSP, from establishing themselves even more firmly in the Diet.

Japanese elections demand a candidate who could win an American primary, i.e., one who can project himself as a desirable candidate from among a field crowded with other nominees of the same party. It would be very worthwhile to compare the personal traits and campaign styles of a JCP, DSP, or CGP candidate, who will always be the only representative of his party running for the Diet in his district, with the candidates and campaigns of the LDP. Or, to introduce a control for party affiliation, these aspects of candidate and campaign could be compared between JSP nominees who are alone in their districts and those who are campaigning with and against other nominees. One study of campaigns in the 1955 election found that leftist candidates more often refer to their party platforms than conservative (LDP) candidates do (Dore 1956). This, of course, fits our expectations, since candidates of the left are more likely to be the only party nominees in their districts.

It would also be worthwhile to compare elections at different levels of government in Japan (local, prefectural, and national), which use different electoral systems. Frequently noted phenomena of Japanese election campaigns, such as the emphasis on the personal (especially the moral) character of the candidate, which seem so incongruous when laid against the realities of national politics in that country, appear to be explicable in terms of the Japanese electoral system.

Appendix

Variable Construction

Coding the Basis of the Vote

The coding of open-ended questions into a manageable number of categories is always a somewhat chancy operation. The best guarantee that the coding scheme employed is both valid and reliable comes when the development of a set of categories is guided by some previous idea or theory of what one is looking for. Fortunately for the validity of the notion that the three basic forces are candidate, issues, and party, most responses in every nation fit these categories very well. In some cases, however, arbitrary choices have to be made as to which of the three categories a given response belongs in. The primary ambiguity arose with broad statements such as "I voted for X (a party or a candidate) because they/he/she favor the working class." These were always coded as issue-oriented responses, although candidate or party content is also very pronounced and one may have serious doubts about the depth of issue awareness that produced them.[18] Other replies which focused on the issues but did not refer also to the candidate were, of course, also coded as issue-oriented responses.

A second case of a rather arbitrary coding rule involves a response that the leader of the party was the prime factor in choosing how to vote. This response, which falls somewhere between party and candidate, occurred primarily in Great Britain and has been coded as a candidate response here. As it happens, nobody in the British survey referred to the local candidate, the person for whom they actually cast their ballots. Responses that referred to the party's national leaders were seen as the equivalent of voting for the candidate in an American presidential election. References to past party leaders, historical figures associated with the party such as Keir Hardie and Winston Churchill, were coded as party-oriented responses.

---

18. There is no reason to believe that putting the joint candidate/issue replies in the issue category introduces any bias or changes any results. Recalculation with these cases in the candidate column would mean a shift of 5 percent from issue to candidate for Japan. This would have made the salience of candidate even more pronounced in Japan relative to the other countries in Table 1.

Such arbitrary decisions do have some effect on the percentage distribution across the categories in each nation. However, the fact that coding decisions were made consistently between nations means that such decisions can have only a marginal effect, if any, on comparisons between nations. Thus the data, though not without limitations, suffice for the purpose at hand.

The Modernity Factor

The following is the result of the factor analysis on the modernity questions:

Variable	Factor 1 (Community)	Factor 2 (Social)	Factor 3 (Emperor)
Have Emperor	.049	-.001	.054
Strengthen Emperor	.116	-.042	.764
Political Emperor	.178	-.022	-.513
Regal Emperor	.147	-.052	-.283
Community Harmony	.729	-.035	.012
Community Solidarity	.719	-.019	.018
Accept Authority	.718	-.016	-.085
Role of Women	.265	.069	.546
Save/Spend Money	-.131	.382	.026
Youth and Discipline	.104	.799	.041
Respect for Parents	.198	.796	.004
Family Solidarity	.237	-.389	-.052
New/Old Type Person	.321	-.230	-.372

It should be noted that the minus signs in the factor scores reflect only the direction in which the various items were coded. Without exception, modern answers on one question are associated with modern answers on other questions in the sample as a whole.

On the basis of this factor analysis, it was decided to drop the first question, on the existence of the emperor, from the Emperor factor. This question does not fit into the factor, probably because of the skewed response to it, with only 7.5 percent saying there should be no emperor in present-day Japan. Also, the results indicated that the question on equality of women conforms better to the Emperor factor than to the Social factor, so it was put in the former.

References

Bernstein, Robert A. 1977. Divisive primaries do hurt: U.S. Senate races, 1956-1972. American Political Science Review, 71:540-45.

Bishop, George F., Alfred J. Tuchfarber, and Robert W. Oldendick. 1978. Change in the structure of American political attitudes: the nagging question of question wording. American Journal of Political Science, 22:250-69.

Campbell, Angus, Philip E. Converse, Warren E. Miller, and Donald E. Stokes. 1960. The American voter. New York: John Wiley.

Converse, Philip E. 1976. The dynamics of party support. Beverly Hills, California: Sage.

Converse, Philip E., and Gregory B. Markus. 1979. Plus ca change. . .: the new CPS election study panel. American Political Science Review, 73:32-49.

Curtis, Gerald L. 1971. Election campaigning Japanese style. New York: Columbia University Press.

De nederlandse kiezer. 1956. The Hague: Staatsdrukkerij.

Dore, R.P. 1956. Japanese election candidates in 1955. Pacific Affairs, 40:14-80.

Flanagan, Scott C. 1968. Voting behavior in Japan. Comparative Political Studies, 1:391-412.

Flanagan, Scott C., and Bradley Richardson. 1977. Japanese electoral behavior: social cleavages, social networks, and partisanship. London: Sage.

Ike, Nobutake. 1972. Japanese politics. New York: Alfred A. Knopf.

Ishida, Takeshi. 1971. Japanese society. New York: Random House.

King, Michael. 1977. Assimilation and contrast of presidential candidates' issue positions, 1972. Public Opinion Quarterly, 41:512-22.

Kubota, Akira. n.d. Party identification and social cleavages in Japan. Unpublished ms.

Nakane, Chie. 1970. Japanese society. Berkeley: University of California Press.

Nie, Norman H., with Kristi Andersen. 1974. Mass belief systems revisited: political change and attitude structure. Journal of Politics, 36:541-91.

Przeworski, Adam, and Henry Teune. 1970. The logic of comparative inquiry. New York: John Wiley.

Reischauer, Edwin. 1978. The Japanese. Cambridge: Harvard University Press.

Richardson, Bradley. 1974. The political culture of Japan. Berkeley: University of California Press.

_____. 1975. Party loyalties and party saliency in Japan. Comparative Political Studies, 8:32-57.

Scalapino, Robert A., and Junnosuke Masumi. 1962. Parties and politics in contemporary Japan. Berkeley: University of California Press.

Sullivan, John L., James F. Piereson, and George E. Marcus. 1978. Ideological constraint in the mass public: a methodological critique and some new findings. American Journal of Political Science, 22:233-49.

Teune, Henry, and Krzysztof Ostrowski. 1973. Political systems as residual variables: explaining differences within systems. Comparative Political Studies, 6:3-27.

Tsurutani, Taketsugu. 1977. Political change in Japan: response to postindustrial change. New York: David McKay.

Ward, Robert E., and Akira Kubota. 1970. Family influence and political socialization in Japan. Comparative Political Studies, 3:140-75.

SOCIAL-ENVIRONMENTAL EFFECTS UPON PARTY ATTACHMENTS: THE CASES OF ITALY AND JAPAN

John Strate

An unfinished task for the field of comparative electoral behavior is to explain why the attachments of some adults to their political party grow stronger while the attachments of others stay the same or grow weaker, and why some adults and not others change their party attachments. What is it in the adult's social environment that leads to either stability or change? Was there anything about the social environment of these individuals when they were growing up that predisposed them to stability or change as an adult? Or is there perhaps some complex interaction between the political experiences of youth and those of an adult that leads them to either stability or change?

These questions are especially important to any understanding of the politics of Italy and Japan. For nearly the entire postwar period in Italy and since 1955 in Japan, a single party has dominated government. However, the grip of the Italian Christian Democrats (DC) and the Japanese Liberal Democratic Party (LDP) has loosened, although for somewhat different reasons. The Italian DC has obtained a fairly constant percentage of the vote (about 38 percent) for more than a decade, but as a minority governing party it has had continuing and increasing difficulty in arranging viable coalitions. In Japan the LDP has lost votes, declining from 57.8 percent in 1958 to 44.6 percent in 1979 (plus 3.0 percent for the New Liberal Club, which split off from the LDP in 1976). Nonetheless, the LDP has managed to hold a majority of the Diet, although by a smaller and smaller margin; in recent years it has been forced to enroll conservative Dietmen actually elected as independents. Differences of electoral system account for much of this contrast: Italy's proportional representation system translates vote percentages almost directly into parliamentary percentages, while Japan's "multi-member, single-ballot, medium-sized electoral district" system, which puts a premium on not "wasting" votes by running too many candidates in a district, tends to favor large parties. Partly because of the tactical skill of its leaders, the LDP has always managed to obtain higher parliamentary than vote percentages, a difference as large as 11.6 percent in the 1967 election.[1] Despite these differences, the DC and the LDP are quite similar. Both are large, conservative parties. Both attempt to draw support from broad sectors of society, but are disproportionately favored by older and more rural citizens. Both, therefore, face the problem of declining support because older people eventually die and because, given the modernization process, the proportion of rural voters has been constantly dropping. The percentage of citizens in Italy who say they are attached to the DC dropped from 42.6 percent in 1968 to 33.8 percent in 1972; in Japan, LDP identifiers dropped from 39.1 percent of the electorate in 1958 to 34.8 percent in 1979.[2] These trends are of crucial importance to the political futures of the two countries, because research has demonstrated that party attachments are the most important component of voting decisions; in most elections they outweigh such short-term forces as issue orientations and evaluations of candidates.[3] Hence it is important to

---

1. Figures for the results of postwar general elections for Japan's House of Representatives are given in Ward (1978:121-25). In the election held in the fall of 1979, the LDP increased its percentage of the vote but ran too many candidates and lost a seat. The June 1980 election saw the LDP increase its share of both votes (to 48 percent) and seats.
2. The percentages for Italy were taken from national sample surveys. The 1968 survey (N = 2,500) was conducted by Samuel Barnes, the University of Michigan. I thank Professor Barnes for the use of his data to construct parts of Tables 1 through 5a. The 1972 survey (N = 1,841) was conducted by Samuel Barnes and Giacomo Sani, Ohio State University. I thank Professors Barnes and Sani for the use of marginal percentages from their survey. Note: a substantial proportion of Italians refuse to answer questions about party attachments. For example, in the 1968 survey 6.5 percent of the respondents did not wish to answer and another 4.5 percent gave no answer. Many of these individuals are probably Communist supporters. The base upon which each DC percentage is computed includes the entire sample, and not just those responding to these questions.

The Japanese percentages are from national sample surveys conducted by the Jiji poll. The data for the Japan portions of Tables 1 through 5b come from a 1967 study conducted by Akira Kubota and Robert Ward which is in the Inter-University Consortium for Political and Social Research (ICPSR) files. The raw N for the adult portion of the study was 1,973. All of the percentages in Tables 1 through 5b, however, are based upon weighted data (weighted N = 21,047). Neither the original collectors of the data nor the ICPSR, which aided in the execution of these surveys, bear any responsibility for the analyses or interpretations presented here.
3. Of course, the relative importance of parties, candidates, and issues for voter choices will vary cross-nationally also, as Thomas Rochon points out in this volume. For the classic statement of this theoretical approach to understanding voting, which was first applied to elections in the United States, see

understand the processes underlying change in the distribution of party attachments. Logically, there are only two such processes: replacement (some citizens die and some enter the electorate), and individual conversion (some citizens acquire an attachment, give up an attachment, or become attached to a different party).

The nature of the decline in party attachments for the DC and the LDP which results from replacement, the first process, has already been well studied in both Italy (Sani and Barnes 1972; Sani 1975b) and Japan (Richardson 1975, 1977). Older people (in particular, those individuals who were already of voting age when World War II came to an end) have been the strongest supporters of the DC and the LDP. They are being replaced in the electorate, however, by the young (those born after World War II, who first entered the electorate in the late 1960s and the 1970s) who of all age groups give the least support to these parties.

There are at least two reasons why a large fraction of older individuals support the DC and the LDP. The major reason is generational. At the end of the war, following a decade or more of fascist and militaristic rule, and because the women among them had not before had the right to vote, most of these individuals were not attached to any political party. For this reason, and because of their mostly rural, apolitical, and socially conservative backgrounds, they were excellent targets for DC and Japanese conservative efforts to mobilize support at the grass-roots level.[4] In the Japanese case another important factor was presumably widespread attachments to conservative factions at the local level, connected to the prewar conservative precursors of the LDP, which continued to be active throughout the war years (Allinson 1975). That the efforts of conservative politicians were very successful is suggested by the large votes obtained in the early post war elections. Such large votes could only be the result of choices by sizeable fractions of these unattached individuals to support the DC and the Japanese conservatives. At that time short-term forces were benefitting these parties. More often than their competitors, these parties possessed the democratic credentials, local organizations, and resources necessary to make

---

Campbell, Converse, Miller, and Stokes (1964). In the United States since the mid-1960s, issues seem to have played an increasingly important role in voter choices—see Nie, Verba, and Petrocik (1976) and also Miller, Miller, Raine, and Brown (1976).
4. The question of why a large fraction of older individuals support the DC and the LDP cannot be answered with direct evidence since there are no survey data available on these points from the immediate postwar years.

such a grass-roots strategy work. The DC used the Catholic Church and its ideology, associations, and resources in an attempt to control the everyday life of Italians (Galli and Prandi 1970). The Japanese conservatives (and later the LDP) relied upon the efforts of locally powerful politicians. These politicians built up close ties to socially important individuals in the hamlets and villages who were able, in machine-like fashion, to mobilize the vote (Curtis 1971; Flanagan 1968, 1971; Ward 1960). A second and less important reason for the continuing support given to these parties, especially to the DC, is the lower mortality rate of older women, who give stronger support to the conservatives than do older men.

To explain the low levels of support given by the young to the DC and the LDP, we need to look at the effects of several forces. At least one force has helped the DC and the LDP, but others have hurt them. The helpful force is partisanship transmission: in both Italy (Sani 1975a) and Japan (Kubota and Ward 1970) parents tend to transmit their own party attachments to their children. Since parents belonging to large parties are most successful in doing this, the parties with the most supporters in their countries (the DC and the LDP) gain an advantage over their smaller competitors. The net effect of this transmission is to greatly lessen the impact of DC and LDP losses due to the deaths of their older supporters, since these individuals were more successful than the older supporters of other parties in transmitting party attachments to their children. Unfortunately for both the DC and the LDP, these older supporters were not wholly successful in transmitting their attachments. A large percentage of their children, perhaps as many as fifty percent, were uncommitted (or independent) when they first became eligible to vote.[5] For this reason, gains due to partisanship transmission do not balance out losses to the DC and the LDP from the deaths of their older supporters. To avoid losing ground the DC and the LDP had to direct appeals to the young who were still uncommitted.

---

5. In the 1972 Italian survey, of those able to recall that their father supported a Catholic party, 78.5 percent supported the DC (Sani 1975a:492). Of those able to recall that their father supported the PCI, 76.5 percent supported the PCI (Sani 1975a:492). The transmission rates are much lower for other parties. In the 1967 Japanese survey there were parent-child pairs: of those children (with a party attachment) whose father supported the LDP, 67.1 percent supported the LDP (Kubota and Ward 1970:148). Of those children (with a party attachment) whose father supported the JSP, 73.1 percent supported the JSP (Kubota and Ward 1970:148). As in Italy, the figures are lower for the smaller parties.

The several harmful forces that depressed DC and LDP support among the young included postwar economic growth and the counter-culture movement of the late 1960s and early 1970s. It both Italy and Japan industrial growth occurred most rapidly in localities where the opposition parties had traditionally been strongest. Thus, many of the young of both Italy and Japan entered new school, workplace, and urban environments that did not encourage DC and LDP attachments. For the young who were already attached to the DC or the LDP, social interaction in such environments would tend to weaken and perhaps erode this prior attachment. For the young who were uncommitted, social interaction in such environments would discourage DC or LDP attachments, and would perhaps lead to attachments with opposition parties. The counter-culture movement had similar effects. Led by a vocal minority of young leftists, the movement was at least partly successful in attacking the leaders and policies of the establishment, which included, of course, the ruling DC and LDP. To some extent the young leftists gained sympathy among others of their generation and large proportions of the young must have acquired a negative image of these parties.[6] To them the DC and the LDP seemed hopelessly corrupt, inept, and reactionary. As parties of pasta and rice, they appeared incapable of dealing with the problems of post-industrial society: economic imperialism, nuclear power and its safety, urban planning, pollution, women's rights, relationships in the workplace, drug abuse, educational opportunity, civil liberties, and terrorism, among others. These negative images were reinforced by incidents of party corruption and malfeasance, such as the Lockheed scandal in Japan.

If these harmful forces persist, support for the DC and the LDP will continue to decline. This will happen because both parties must make up for losses due to deaths by gaining more support among the young who, despite the negative images they may currently hold of these parties, still include a disproportionate fraction of those in the electorate who are still open to conversion. The conservative parties will have difficulty in doing this. While they are experienced in the old tactics of organizational politics, these methods do not always reach the young of post-industrial society. The young do not have their parents' strong ties to industrial, interest-group, labor, religious, and residential organizations and they do not see why their

---

6. There are no party image data for Italy of the "open-ended" variety that would let us test this hypothesis. There are some party image data from the 1967 Japanese survey, however, and they do show that the young held a more negative image of the LDP—see my unpublished paper "Alternative Approaches to the Understanding of a Complex Voter: The Case of Japan." See also Flanagan and Richardson (1980).

organizational memberships should bind them politically. Also, they are often less interested in politics than their parents, in spite of their greater education.[7] For this reason they will depend more heavily than their parents upon television and other passive sources for political information and opinion. The DC and the LDP, with their aging leadership, however, may find the mass media difficult to use effectively. The "catch-all" electoral strategy of trying to please everybody while alienating nobody may simply not work with young people who expect parties to address political issues directly. So the DC and the LDP face a dilemma. To insure a future for themselves as ruling parties they must gain the support of more young voters. To do so, however, may require the sorts of changes in outlook and policy that will cause the parties to fracture internally, as happened in Japan in 1976 when the New Liberal Club left the LDP. It is therefore questionable whether the DC and the LDP will be able to implement the strategies necessary to insure a sufficient number of conversions to themselves to offset the losses due to replacement. To understand how the distribution of party attachments in these countries is likely to change in the future, we need to examine the processes of conversion observable in the past.

Social Environments and Party Attachments

The causes of stability and change in party attachments, in Italy and Japan as elsewhere, are ultimately social-environmental. This has been evident from the earliest voting studies. The first of these, The People's Choice (Lazarfeld, Berelson, and Gaudet 1948), was able to associate patterns of political communications (the "two-step flow") with the tendency toward partisan homogeneity within social groups. In the second of these studies, Voting (Berelson, Lazarsfeld, and McPhee 1954), it was found that individuals who were cross-pressured (or, in other words, were predisposed by their social group memberships in different partisan directions) tended to delay making a decision on how to vote, and more often voted contrary to their party attachments. In another study, Miller (1956) found that minority parties suffered disproportionate losses in localities where they trailed far behind. In these localities the minority party faced an uphill battle in recruiting good

---

7. For a comparative analysis of participation and the life cycle see Nie, Verba and Kim (1974). The authors find that participation is lowest among the youngest age group, and remarkably low considering that the youngest age group has much more education, which is almost everywhere correlated positively with rates of participation.

candidates, building an organization, and campaigning, since its prospects for electoral success were so slim. A landmark publication, The American Voter (Campbell et al. 1964), showed that the length of time an individual has belonged to a group determined the probable influence of that group on the individual's political orientations. It also found that changes in party attachment which occurred for purely personal reasons usually involved a change in the individual's social environment due to a marriage, a new job, or a change of residence. A secondary analysis of survey data by Putnam (1966) showed that active participation in a group was linked to increased susceptibility to the influence of the group members. If a given party held a slight balance of support among the active residents of a community (those who tend to be disproportionately active in community social groups), this party would hold a much larger balance of support among these social groups. Finally, a study of factory-floor-level friendship groups among auto workers in the Detroit area showed that individuals tend to select groups with partisan views close to their own (Finifter 1974).

For the most part, the studies of party attachments in Italy and Japan have only been able to look at the effects of social environments indirectly. Survey results from Italy (Barnes 1974; Sani 1974, 1975b) were able to demonstrate the cumulative effect of such factors as church attendance, Catholic union vs. leftist union, occupational status, and local political traditions upon attachment to the DC. Survey results from Japan (Watanuki 1967; Flanagan and Richardson 1977) were able to demonstrate the cumulative effects of such factors as union vs. non-union, occupation, size of enterprise, home ownership vs. rental, length of residence, sex, and age upon the level of LDP voting and the level of attachment to the LDP (or conservative parties). Recently there has been increasing interest in contextual effects upon partisanship. In Italy, Sani (1976) looked at the effects of separate leftist and Catholic subcultures upon the stability of individual party attachments. He found that homogeneous social environments encouraged stability in party attachments while heterogeneous social environments did not. The impact of contextual factors upon partisanship occurred largely through the increased likelihood that individuals living in any particular locality would belong to an organization tied into one of the party networks. The study mentioned above by Flanagan and Richardson (1977) noted that "social networks" should be especially important in a hierarchically organized society like Japan. They found that the partisan characteristics of the workplace are as important as those of the home in Japan, unlike the case in Italy. A study by White (1973) of rural migrants showed a degree of anticipatory socialization. The partisan characteristics of rural migrants more nearly resembled those of the people of the urban areas to which they had moved than those of the areas they had left.

The work to date on contextual effects has yet to set out and test in any confident way a theory of how social environments lead to partisan stability or change. There seem to be only two general findings: 1) the effects of influence within social environments are additive, so that homogeneous social environments lead to partisan stability and heterogeneous social environments to partisan instability (the "cross-pressure" hypothesis), and 2) the effects of social environments upon partisanship depend upon actual social interaction (it is what individuals do and say with others that matters).

These studies, unfortunately, are not based upon a general theory that links processes of social influence to the individual's attachment to a party. In particular, the approaches used to date fail to recognize the possibility that there are two dimensions of partisanship—strength and durability—and that these might vary independently. These social scientists assume that if an individual is strongly attached to a party, that attachment will persist, and if an individual is only weakly attached, the attachment may well not persist. This assumption may flow from the wording of the questions used in most surveys to ascertain partisanship. A respondent is often asked to estimate how durable his commitment has been to a party: for example, in the 1968 Italian survey, "To which party do you habitually feel closest?" It is far better to define strength in behavioral terms: as the frequency/intensity with which individuals show their support for a party verbally. Strictly speaking, this dimension could be measured only by direct observation of the frequency/intensity of an individual's political conversations, which of course would be difficult. From this perspective the act of voting (and other manifestations of partisanship) is seen as a distinct behavior. Of course, strength of attachment will usually correlate with stable party voting, but if the two are actually distinct behaviors, it need not always do so.

A second dimension of party attachment, I would argue, is its durability. It would seem on the face of it that the best indicator of the durability of an attachment would be its persistence over time. This measurement, however, ignores entirely an important feature of all social behaviors, like party attachments, which are learned. This feature—which will be the definition of durability used here—is the persistence of a behavior after the behavior ceases to be socially rewarded (or reinforced). For how long does the individual maintain the frequency/intensity of verbal support for a party even though this behavior is no longer accepted or encouraged by others?

According to behavioral theory, the most important factor affecting the probable durability of any given behavior is the functional need for it to endure. At one extreme are behaviors, such as reflexes, which in certain types of situations always need to be performed in the same fashion and so must always be a part of the individual's repertoire. When we cough because an object is caught in our windpipe it is because the nerves and muscles that enable such behavior were favored by natural selection. They must do the job in the same way, every time. At an intermediate position are behaviors which need to be performed differently from time to time, but not so differently that we need to learn them over again each time. Examples include the motor skills used in sports, such as the jump shot in basketball and the service in tennis. At the other extreme are behaviors, such as some social behaviors, which not only must adjust as the individual changes roles, but must also be flexible enough to meet the unique contingencies of different settings. For example, the way a man greets his boss is usually different from the way he greets his wife; indeed, the greeting he gives either may depend on where he is, whether he is late or not, whether others are nearby, and other aspects of the specific setting.[8]

I would argue that party attachments fall into this latter category. The susceptibility of these attachments to social reinforcement in the family, the school, the peer group, the workplace, and the social group suggest that they function to provide the individual with a social identity in the world of politics. They help the individual to adjust to the politically relevant contingencies of the immediate social environment. This is necessary if the individual is to use the social environment to his own best advantage. If this hypothesis is correct, the durability of party attachments should depend upon all of the factors which affect the durability of other sorts of flexible, learned, social behaviors.

Crucial among these factors is the timing of prior reinforcement. It is known from experiments that behaviors will persist for only a short time after a period of <u>regular</u> reinforcement (reinforcement that occurs each time the behavior occurs), if such reinforcement stops. An example would be the adjustments that an individual makes after a change in a daily routine. At first, through "force of habit," the individual may sleep through the alarm clock, or show up by mistake in old places at the old times, but he will not do this for long. It is also known from experiments that behaviors will persist for a long time if reinforcement stops after a period of <u>irregular</u> reinforcement. An example is the novice poker player who wins a few intermittent hands through sheer luck, and soon starts throwing money into every pot even though his

---

8. For views of learning as a biological adaptation, see Bitterman (1975) and Alexander (1975).

luck, and his cards, have soured. These generalizations about the causes of durability of learned behavior have been repeatedly confirmed by experiments in behavioral psychology (Skinner and Ferster 1957), but their implications for party attachments have not been explored. In short, the implications are that in groups with heterogeneous partisanship, where only occasional reinforcement is given for particular partisan views, the party attachments of individuals should be quite durable. In groups which are partisanly homogeneous, and therefore regularly reinforce particular partisan views, the party attachments of individuals should be less durable.

Although this definition of durability may seem odd, its value is clear in light of the frustration experienced in recent years by those investigating party attachments from a conventional viewpoint, when they attempt to explain the substantial changes in such attachments which have recently occurred in several countries. The sharp declines in levels of partisanship which have occurred in the Netherlands (Lijphart 1974) and the United States (Converse 1976; Campbell 1977), for example, illustrate the hazards of estimating the stability of party attachments on the basis of their strength, or for that matter on their stability in the past.

The proposed redefinition of "strength" involves a quite different view of what a party attachment really is. In most conceptualizations a party attachment takes on special status as an "attitude"; it is internalized, and on that account, is able by itself to affect other political attitudes and behaviors. If party attachments are stripped of this special status, however, and viewed simply as a form of verbal behavior (whether overt, as in conversation, or covert, as in thinking), a much different perspective emerges on the sorts of events which are likely to lead to a strengthening, a weakening, or a change of individual party attachments. An unusual feature of verbal behavior, one which sets it apart from other forms of learned behavior, is that its development tends to be not so often or so immediately subject to environmental contingencies (Skinner 1974:88-90). For most non-verbal behaviors there is usually immediate and unambiguous feedback about performance. For example, if the novice bicyclist does not pedal fast enough, the bicycle will tip over. With verbal behavior, on the other hand, there are many occasions when feedback is not so immediate or its significance so clearcut.

Take the following example. Suppose that an individual belongs to a social group, would like to talk about politics, but does not know which party (or parties) the other members support. If the individual does talk about politics, he may manage to alienate one or more of the members who disagree with him. If these members laugh or become angry, feedback functions much like it does for other non-verbal behaviors. It is immediate and its meaning unambiguous. The individual, if he is not too argumentative, will probably save himself from further embarrassment by keeping quiet. If, however, these other members say nothing at that moment, or do not say how they actually feel, feedback is much different. It is less immediate and more ambiguous, and the effect on the individual's behavior may be unpredictable. The individual may act as if "nothing said" indicates support for his viewpoint, and continue talking. Or he may act as if "nothing said" indicates opposition, and stop talking. Or, of course, he may find the situation confusing and not know what to do. What is important to note is that the way the individual acts in this particular situation is likely to depend on what has happened to him in similar situations in the past. And depending on how others react, either reinforcing or failing to reinforce his actions, his attachment may grow either stronger or weaker. The same sorts of social interactions might cause an individual to abandon a party attachment, or to take up a new one. For this reason, a strengthening, weakening, or change in an individual's party attachment is a product of both past social environments (inasmuch as the individual's current behavior is a product of a unique developmental history, which has placed constraints upon the tempo and direction of possible subsequent change) and of the present social environment (where the contingencies of social reinforcement are present to provide the proximate stimulus for a change in the individual's behavior).

If the situation is this complex, the theory suggested above will be difficult indeed to test. One major implication is that the behavior an individual displays at any moment has meaning only if it is understood within the context of his particular learning history. To explain the strength of any given individual's party attachment, it would be necessary to identify how various features of the social environments to which he has been exposed in the past have structured the patterns by which his partisan views were socially reinforced. What were the contingencies of reinforcement which had an impact on implanting, sustaining, or changing the individual's party attachments?

Pursuing the implications of the voting studies cited above, I hypothesize that a critical factor determining these contingencies of reinforcement is the relative partisan homogeneity/heterogeneity of the individual's social environment. Are the political communications of a particular social environment overwhelmingly favorable to a single party (or ideological tendency), or do they conflict? The former situation defines a social environment where partisan talk is mostly homogeneous, and reinforcement regular; in the latter situation partisan talk is mostly heterogeneous, and reinforcement irregular.

To examine the impact of different types of social environments upon party attachments, I have classified individuals, from both the Italian and Japanese samples, according to the relative partisan homogeneity/heterogeneity of the social environments they experienced both as children and as adults. That is, in coding the relative partisan homogeneity/heterogeneity of the initial social environments of the Italians, the partisan directions of four variables were considered: the ideological direction of the father's party attachment (left, none, right); attendance at a church school (no, yes); father's occupation (working class, farm, middle class); and the ideological characteristics of the region of origin (left, heterogeneous, right). For Japan, the variables are the party attachment, social class, occupation of the father, and the region of origin. If all factors were supportive of a rightist party attachment, the initial social environment was coded as right-homogeneous. If all factors were supportive of a leftist party attachment, the initial social environment was coded as left-homogeneous. When the factors were unbalanced, but mixed, the initial social environment was coded either as right-heterogeneous or left-heterogeneous, as appropriate. Only in cases where the factors were exactly balanced was the initial social environment coded as heterogeneous. Therefore, there are five categories of initial social environments.

The "final" or current environments of the respondents were similarly classified. For Italy, the variables are union membership, church attendance, class, and partisan composition of region; for Japan, they are union membership, class, occupation, and partisan composition of the electoral district.

The details of this coding scheme are contained in the appendix. Table 1 shows the percentages of the Italian and Japanese samples placed in the coding categories according to the above scheme.[9] It shows, as expected, that very few individuals in either Italy or Japan spent their childhoods in a social environment that was left-homogeneous. The partisan character of the

---

9. See Appendix for the coding strategy. In order to insure a large enough sample for cross-tabulation, all respondents were classified based upon whatever information was available for them. This undoubtedly leads to the misclassification of a few cases. For example, an Italian who had a father who supported the Populist Party, but who could not recall that fact in 1968, might be classified on the basis of other information as growing up in a left-homogeneous or a left-heterogeneous environment, whereas in fact the environment was heterogeneous. Such errors should decrease the strength of observed relationships. I felt that the problem of sample attenuation due to the presence of missing data would be far more serious than the problem resulting from the misclassification of a few respondents.

TABLE 1
Change in Partisan Environments, Italy and Japan

A. Italy

Environment as Adult	L.Hom	Environment as Youth				Total	N
		L.Het	Heter	R.Het	R.Hom		
L.Hom	1.0%[a]	1.1%	2.5%	.4%	.1%	5.2%	129
L.Het	1.2	3.0	9.0	6.7	4.9	24.8	621
Heter	.2	1.9	6.7	11.1	9.6	29.6	739
R.Het	.4	2.4	6.4	14.0	13.4	36.6	915
R.Hom	0.0	.4	.2	1.2	2.1	3.8	96
Total	2.9%	8.7%	24.8%	33.4%	30.2%	100.0%	
N	73	217	621	835	754		2500

B. Japan

Environment as Adult	L.Hom	Environment as Youth				Total	N
		L.Het	Heter	R.Het	R.Hom		
L.Hom	-[b]	-	-	-	-	-	-
L.Het	-	5.2%[c]	5.6%	10.2%	3.5%	24.5%	481
Heter	-	4.6	11.4	18.5	7.7	42.1	821
R.Het	-	1.2	3.2	16.7	6.8	27.8	561
R.Hom	-	.1	0.0	3.5	1.9	5.5	110
Total	-	11.1%	20.2%	48.9%	19.8%	99.9%	
N (Raw)	-	212	403	969	389		1973

Notes:
   a. Each entry is the percent of the total sample who experienced environmental change of a particular type.
   b. There are no individuals in left-homogeneous environments in Japan
   c. The percentages for Japan are based on data which were weighted; weighted N = 21,047.

Code: L.Hom = Left-homogeneous; L.Het = Left-heterogeneous; Heter = Heterogeneous; R.Het = Right-heterogeneous; R.Hom = Right-homogeneous.

initial social environments of most of these individuals was either mostly apolitical or leaning towards the right. A substantial fraction of individuals from both countries, however, were living as adults within social environments which were at least partially supportive of an attachment with a leftist party. This is to be expected given the historical processes of industrialization, urbanization, and secularization in both Italy and Japan. Table 1 shows that the partisan character of individuals' social environments has changed substantially for large fractions of both Italians and Japanese. As will be shown later, these changes in the partisan homgeneity/heterogeneity of social environments can significantly affect the readiness with which party attachments are acquired, the strength with which they are held, and the likelihood of their changing.

It is also interesting to note the percentage of individuals within each of the cells that at the time of the survey identified with a party on the left (for Italy) or with a party other than the LDP (for Japan), and the percentage of individuals that identified with a party on the right (for Italy) or with the LDP (for Japan). Figure 1 presents these percentages. It demonstrates several things.

First, it is evident that both the partisan environment of youth and the partisan environment of adulthood have had an impact upon party affiliation. The marginal percentages (total columns and rows) show substantial differences in both dimensions. The sharpest differences, in both Italy and Japan, occur between heterogeneous and left-heterogeneous environments. It seems that the likelihood of support for a party on the left increases greatly if there is any imbalance, whether as a youth or as an adult, in the social-environmental forces favoring the left. On the other hand, the likelihood of support for a party on the right seems to increase with the relative homogeneity of forces in the youthful environment that supported such an attachment, so long as the forces of the adult environment are not imbalanced in favor of the left. The net impression is what one might expect. The parties of the right, in both Italy and Japan, are beneficiaries of historical conditions that once imparted to youths an outlook that was socially and politically conservative. The forces of industrialization, urbanization, and secularization have slowly eroded these former advantages. They have created social environments that support political attachments with parties of the left.

Second, it is evident that there are substantial numbers of deviants, that is, individuals who as adults hold party attachments that are not compatible with the dominant partisan characteristics of their adult social environments. Deviancy appears to diminish as the partisan characteristics of the

FIGURE 1. The Impact of Social Environments on Partisanship

A. ITALY   PARTISAN ENVIRONMENT AS A YOUTH
Percent Who Identify with a Party of the Left or Right[a]

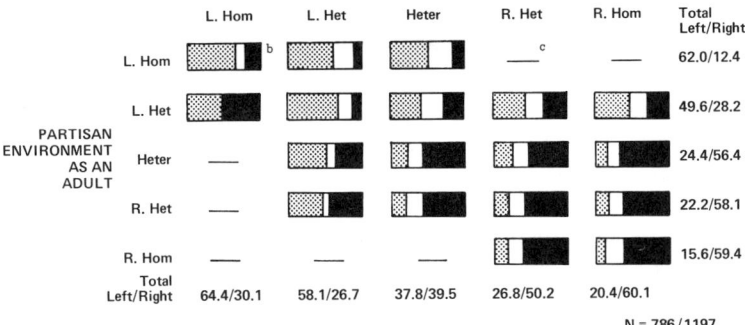

B. JAPAN   PARTISAN ENVIRONMENT AS A YOUTH
Percent Who Identify with a Party of the Left or Right[d]

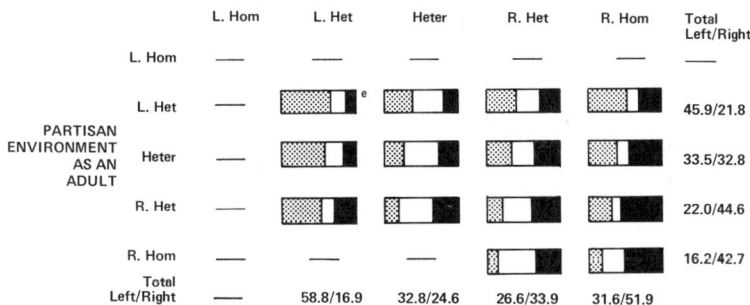

Notes:
a. For Italy, parties of the left include the PCI, the PSIUP, the PSU, and the PRI; parties of the right include the DC, the PLI, MON, and MSI.
b. The total length of each bar is equivalent to 100 percent; the light-shaded portion of each bar to the left is for the parties of the left, the unshaded center portion of each bar includes no answers, null responses, others, independents, and don't knows, and the dark-shaded portion of each bar to the right is for the parties of the right.
c. Percentages were not computed (i.e., a bar does not appear) for cells or marginals where the total number of individuals, or the base upon which the percentages were computed, was less than 25.
d. For Japan, parties of the left include the JCP, CGP, JSP, and DSP; parties of the right include the LDP.
e. The percentages for Japan are based upon data which were weighted; weighted N for the left identifiers is equal to 6,646; weighted N for LDP identifiers is 6,959.

adult social environment become increasingly hostile, or more homogeneous in a hostile direction, but never vanishes entirely. The likelihood of being a deviant partisan is considerably enhanced, of course, if such a deviant attachment was actually the predominant attachment in the youthful social environment.

Third, it is also evident that the effects of different partisan environments are not always monotonic and additive. For example, it seems to make little difference, in either Italy or Japan, whether an individual grew up within a right-heterogeneous or a heterogeneous environment. With few exceptions, the differences in percentages across these two columns are quite small. This indicates that individuals who grew up in these environments have similar partisan characteristics when they reach adulthood (controlling, of course, for the partisan characteristics of the adult social environment). Still more interesting is the contrast between these individuals and those who grew up within a right-homogeneous environment. The level of support given by those who grew up in a right-homogeneous environment to parties on the right seems to depend very much on the partisan characteristics of the adult social environment, whereas the levels of support given by those who grew up in either a right-heterogeneous environment or a heterogeneous environment do not. Such a difference might be expected if the stability of party attachments depended on the way in which they were learned during youth. The existence of such effects, which involve interaction, necessarily complicates any explanation of partisan change, and ultimately affects our understanding of the distribution of party support.

To simplify the presentation of my explanation I will handle it in parts. I will first try to explain how the partisan characteristics of the social environments of youths can affect whether or not they acquire a party attachment, and if they do, which attachment they acquire. I will next try to demonstrate how rates of partisan change, or the likelihood that an individual will switch out of a particular party is affected in complicated ways by the partisan characteristics of the social environments of both youth and adulthood. Finally, I will look at the ways in which partisan characteristics of the adult social environment affect the strength of partisanship and, as a digression, will present some cross-national evidence on strength of partisanship that supports this argument.

The Acquisition of Party Attachments

The most important factor facilitating the acquisition of party attachments by children is the existence of party attachments by their parents. Studies from a number of countries have shown that children, at a very young age, are able to indicate a preference for a party, and that this preference is usually the same as that of their parents (Dennis and McCrone 1970). This is also true of Italy (Sani 1975a) and Japan (Kubota and Ward 1970). In these two countries, however, partly because of the interlude of fascism and militarism, only a small fraction (26.9 percent of Italians; 36.7 percent of Japanese) can recall their father's partisanship, if any.[10] For this reason the party attachments of parents have been less important in shaping the overall distribution of party support in these two countries than in countries like Great Britain and the United States where such disruptions of the party system did not occur.

A number of findings concerning this transmission process suggest that it occurs through social learning. Such learning can occur at a very young age, and it is evident that this is true of party attachments, which children acquire as early as 6 or 7 years of age (Easton and Dennis 1969). These attachments seem to serve purposes similar to those served by other sorts of social identifications acquired at an early age—for example, social class, race, and religion—which provide children with an unambiguous means of sorting out their family's position in a larger but as yet undifferentiated world. That this process constitutes social learning is suggested by other facts. Children acquire attachments most often when parents hold the same partisanship, when the family talks frequently about politics, and when children are close to their parents (Converse and Dupeux 1962; Jennings and Niemi n.d.). When fathers and mothers disagree, children more often take up the partisanship of their mothers, probably because children interact more frequently with their mothers and tend to like them better than they do their fathers (Jennings and Niemi n.d.).

The finding concerning mothers' influence indicates that caution is necessary whenever the father's party is used as a summary description of the partisan environment of the home. Fortunately, this is less of a problem for Italy and Japan than it is for a country like the United States. At the time survey respondents were growing up, the families of Italy (Sani 1974) and

---

10. Percentages computed from the Barnes 1968 survey and the Kubota-Ward 1967 survey.

Japan (Kubota and Ward 1970) were overwhelmingly partisan-homogeneous. Furthermore, married women in these countries probably relied more heavily on their husbands for political direction than did married women in the United States. Family structure in these countries was more authoritarian and in both Italy and Japan women have historically been excluded from political life. For these reasons, the father's party is probably a good indicator of the partisan environment of the home.

Although the impact of parents upon party attachments is surely predominant, there are other factors in the social environments of children that may have some effects. Important agents of political socialization include neighbors, friends, schools, siblings, and the mass media. The influence of these agents may either reinforce the parental transmission process or counteract it. For example, in Italy the transmission of a DC party attachment is probably reinforced by a Catholic elementary education. However, for children of DC parents living in the Red Belt region, the leftist inclinations of the newspapers, labor unions, and local political parties may counteract DC transmission. In Japan the transmission of an LDP party attachment would be reinforced for children living in prefectures where the LDP candidates win elections handily and sweep most of the seats. It would be counteracted if the father happened to belong to a labor union, since many of the neighbors and friends of the family would probably be supporters of the Japan Socialist Party (JSP).

In general, as the partisan character of a child's social environment becomes more heterogeneous, it should be increasingly difficult for the child to acquire an attachment that is compatible with the dominant partisan tendency of that environment. Indeed, as the social environment becomes more heterogeneous, it becomes less and less likely that regular reinforcement will occur for any partisan behavior. As a consequence, the child may fail to acquire any sort of attachment, whether it is compatible with the dominant partisan tendency or not. This can happen because behaviors which are just being learned usually require a period of regular reinforcement to gain a foothold. For example, we often forget the name of a person to whom we have just been introduced; it is only after we have interacted with people socially for some time, and have some reason to remember them, that we easily recall their names.

Table 2 shows the effects of the homogeneity/heterogeneity of partisan forces in the initial social environments of Italians and Japanese upon their degree of susceptibility to party attachments that are compatible with the partisan direction of these environments. In general, the strong relationship

TABLE 2
The Effect of the Homogeneity/Heterogeneity of the Partisan
Environment of Youth Upon Initial Party Attachments

A. Italy

	\multicolumn{5}{c}{Environment as Youth}				
	L.Hom	L.Het	Heter	R.Het	R.Hom
1) Picked up compatible attachment % Left or (Right)[a]	67.1	57.1		(50.1)	(60.1)
2) Deviant attachment % Left or (Right)	(27.4)	(27.6)		27.7	21.6
3) Grew up in heterogeneous environment % Identifying Left % Identifying (Right)			39.5 (38.8)		
4) Ratio (Right) / Left	.41	.48	.98	1.8	2.8
5) % who picked up any sort of attachment (1+2+3)[b]	94.5	84.7	78.3	77.7	81.7
6) Sample sizes[c]	73	217	621	835	754

B. Japan

	\multicolumn{5}{c}{Environment as Youth}				
	L.Hom	L.Het	Heter	R.Het	R.Hom
1) Picked up compatible attachment % Left or (Right)	–	60.1[d]		(34.7)	(52.7)
2) Deviant attachment % Left or (Right)	–	(14.7)		25.0	29.6
3) Grew up in heterogeneous environment % Identifying Left % Identifying (Right)			31.7 (25.1)		
4) Ratio (Right) / Left	–	.24	.79	1.4	1.8
5) % who picked up any sort of attachment (1+2+3)	–	74.8	56.8	59.7	82.3
6) Sample sizes (raw N)[e]		212	341	969	389

Notes:
a. Party identifications are initial identifications, before any switches have occurred.
b. Base upon which percentage is computed includes "no answers" and "null responses."
c. Sample sizes are bases upon which percentages are computed.
d. The percentages for Japan are based on data which were weighted.
e. Corresponding weighted Ns are 4,174, 10,293, 3,706, and 2,333.

between early environment and initial partisan attachment is again clearly demonstrated. Our further expectation is that a higher proportion of individuals who spent their youth in homogeneously partisan environments would have picked up attachments compatible with that environment than would individuals who spent their youth in more heterogeneous environments. The figures confirm this expectation. Of those growing up in a right-homogeneous environment, 60.1 percent of the Italians and 52.7 percent of the Japanese identified initially with a party on the right; however, for those growing up in right-heterogeneous environments, only 50.1 percent and 34.7 percent respectively identified initially with a party on the right. Similarly, in Italy, of those growing up in a left-homogeneous environment, 67.1 percent identified initially with a party on the left; for those growing up in a left-heterogeneous environment, only 57.1 percent identified initially with a party on the left.

Table 2 also shows the extent to which growing up in a heterogeneous environment inhibits susceptibility to any sort of party attachment. Among Italians who grew up in a heterogeneous environment, 78.3 percent managed to pick up an attachment; for the Japanese, the figure is 56.8 percent. These percentages are substantially less than the percentages for those growing up in homogeneous environments.

These figures also point to the interesting fact that a much higher proportion of Italians (80.2 percent) than Japanese (65.5 percent) claimed to have at least once been attached to a political party. Unlike Japan, in Italy the partisan character of the early social environments seems to have had little impact on people's subsequent ability to pick up party attachments.

There is, incidentally, a potential explanation for this divergence. It relates to postwar differences in party strategy between the two countries and differences in their electoral laws. Party elites in Italy, more so than in Japan, have invested enormous energy and resources into recruiting ordinary people into their organizational folds. As Galli and Prandi (1970) have shown, this has especially been the case for the DC and the PCI (Italian Communist Party) elites. As a result, the Italian political parties have been highly visible political objects in the postwar period. A study by Barnes (1971), for example, showed that most Italians are knowledgeable enough to align the parties correctly along the left-right spectrum. In Japan, on the other hand, the organizational efforts of elites have taken a slightly different form. The unusual electoral system has been largely responsible. A system where individuals cast a single ballot in a multi-member district for a single candidate, and where the ballots are not aggregated by party, forces candidates from the same parties, as competitors, to de-emphasize party in their campaigns, and to emphasize their personal qualities and local ties. As a consequence, the local organizational efforts of the parties have largely been the responsibility of individual candidates (Curtis 1971). The Japanese electorate, for its part, must focus on candidates or issues, rather than on parties, especially in those districts where the parties are running more than a single candidate, for these are the districts where voters pay the most attention to candidates (see Rochon, this volume). Partisanship in Japan has not fused with the social structure to the degree that it has in Italy. For this reason, a much smaller percentage of Japanese than of Italians who were of voting age at the end of World War II eventually acquired party attachments. If this interpretation is the correct one, the proof will lie in examination of additional countries with different party and electoral systems.

Change in Party Attachments

The above discussion satisfactorily accounts for the presence or absence of party attachments and their direction. It does not speak to their quality which, as noted above, should be seen as the separate characteristics of durability and strength. Durability refers to the persistence of a party attachment after social reinforcement for it stops—individuals with more durable attachments are less likely to lose them as the social environment becomes more hostile to their attachment. Durability can be measured directly, since the surveys include questions that ask respondents which parties, if any, they had supported earlier.[11] Tables 3 and 4 present the "defection rates" for the (potential) twenty-five groups of respondents which result from crossing the five childhood and five adult (or final) environments, divided into those who had initially supported the right and the left in each country.

---

11. There are a number of problems in trying to identify the social-environmental causes of change in individual party attachments. If cross-sectional data are used, as we have done, there is the problem of recall: some individuals who have changed parties will forget that they have done so, and some who have not changed parties will think that they have. Unfortunately, the substitution of panel data is not a panacea. Panel data often span only a four or six year period, while changes in party attachments can occur at any time in the life cycle. The changes that are observed in a panel, therefore, will be only a limited proportion of those that might be expected to occur if the individuals in the panel were followed throughout their lives.

TABLE 3
Social Environmental Effects
Upon Partisanship Stability: Italy

A. Percent Switching Out of Those Initially Identifying with a Party on the Right[a]

Partisan Environment as Adult	Partisan Environment as a Youth					
	L.Hom	L.Het	Heter	R.Het	R.Hom	Total
L.Hom	-	-	-	-	-	-
L.Het	-	-	1.7 (59)[b]	10.5 (57)	8.6 (35)	6.3 (175)
Heter	-	-	3.3 (90)	2.1 (141)	1.8 (169)	2.2 (414)
R.Het	-	11.5 (26)	4.8 (84)	4.0 (202)	5.6 (216)	5.1 (533)
R.Hom	-	-	-	-	3.0 (33)	5.5 (55)
Total	-	8.5 (59)	3.7 (241)	4.3 (418)	4.2 (453)	Overall = 4.3 (1192)

B. Percent Switching Out of Those Initially Identifying with a Party on the Left[c]

Partisan Environment as Adult	Partisan Environment as a Youth					
	L.Hom	L.Het	Heter	R.Het	R.Hom	Total
L.Hom	-	-	0.0 (40)[d]	-	-	2.5 (81)
L.Het	-	1.9 (53)	3.7 (108)	5.6 (72)	5.0 (60)	3.9 (310)
Heter	-	3.8 (26)	6.1 (49)	8.5 (71)	13.5 (37)	8.0 (188)
R.Het	-	3.6 (28)	21.3 (47)	13.3 (75)	17.2 (58)	14.5 (214)
R.Hom	-	-	-	-	-	-
Total	4.1 (49)	2.4 (124)	6.9 (245)	9.5 (231)	12.9 (163)	Overall = 8.3 (812)

Overall Percentage of switchers for Italy = 5.6

Notes:
  a. Those who "switched out" either abandoned their partisanship or acquired an attachment with a party on the left.
  b. Figures for sample sizes represent the number of individuals who initially identified with a party on the right and experienced a particular type of environmental change; cells with less than 25 cases are not presented.
  c. Those who "switched out" either abandoned their partisanship or acquired an attachment with a party on the right.
  d. Figures for sample sizes represent the number of individuals who initially identified with a party on the left and experienced a particular type of environmental change; cells with less than 25 cases are not presented.

TABLE 4
Social Environmental Effects
Upon Partisanship Stability: Japan

A. Percent of Those Initially Identifying with the LDP Who Gave Up Their Partisanship or Switched to an Opposition Party[a]

Partisan Environment as Adult	Partisan Environment as a Youth					
	L.Hom	L.Het	Heter	R.Het	R.Hom	Total
L.Hom	-	-	-	-	-	-
L.Het	-	-	8.7[b] (21)[c]	12.1 (53)	19.5 (23)	13.1 (111)
Heter	-	-	4.2 (46)	7.6 (115)	9.2 (76)	8.1 (254)
R.Het	-	-	-	14.3 (139)	10.3 (83)	9.0 (246)
R.Hom	-	-	-	3.7 (27)	13.8 (21)	8.0 (49)
Total	-	18.3 (37)	6.6 (86)	7.7 (334)	11.2 (203)	Overall = 9.3 (660)

B. Percent of Those Initially Identifying With an Opposition Party Who Gave Up Their Partisanship or Switched to the LDP

Partisan Environment as Adult	Partisan Environment as a Youth					
	L.Hom	L.Het	Heter	R.Het	R.Hom	Total
L.Hom	-	-	-	-	-	-
L.Het	-	4.3 (62)[d]	8.2 (46)	17.9 (75)	27.4 (36)	13.4 (219)
Heter	-	1.9 (50)	8.1 (58)	10.8 (113)	15.5 (46)	9.4 (267)
R.Het	-	-	-	15.0 (65)	24.9 (35)	15.1 (122)
R.Hom	-	-	-	-	-	-
Total	-	2.9 (125)	7.4 (115)	14.4 (263)	23.3 (123)	Overall = 9.2 (626)

Overall percentage of switchers for Japan = 9.2

Notes:
    a. Opposition parties include the DSP, the JSP, CGP, and the JCP.
    b. The percentages are based upon data which were weighted.
    c. Figures for sample sizes represent the number of individuals who initially identified with the LDP and experienced a particular type of environmental change; sample sizes are the raw N; cells with less than 20 cases are not presented.
    d. Figures for sample sizes represent the number of individuals who initially identified with an opposition party and experienced a particular type of environmental change; sample sizes are the raw N; cells with less than 20 cases are not presented.

Although the existing literature does not speak directly to this point, it implies that the more favorable the initial environment, the stronger the attachment to a party. For example, a child who is exposed only to right-wing communications, and who is regularly reinforced for supporting such views, should have a stronger attachment to a right-wing party than a child who is exposed to conflicting or left-wing communications, and who is not regularly reinforced for supporting right-wing views. Since the strength of attachments should be highly correlated with their durability, we would expect that the results for the Total (bottom) rows of Tables 3 and 4 would be monotonic: the likelihood of defecting from one's initial party attachment should increase continuously as the amount of exposure to opposing party influence during youth increases. This is not the case except perhaps for Table 4B (where we lack cases for a left-homogeneous initial environment and cannot make a fair assessment). Clearly, a more complex explanation to predict the likelihood of abandoning an initial party attachment is required. The fact that in these bottom rows low defection rates are associated with more heterogeneous initial environments indicates that our learning theory interpretation outlined above may make sense.

That is, we argue that a party attachment should be abandoned, as are other behaviors, when it fails over an extended period of time to receive social reinforcement. Although the act of giving up an attachment is discrete and instantaneous, it is likely that the strength of the attachment, because of the absence of social reinforcement, will have declined considerably before the attachment is actually and finally abandoned. As this occurs, the person will indicate support for his party less frequently and less vigorously in social conversation. The rate at which this happens—or, in other words, the attachment's durability—can be quite variable. Some attachments will lose their strength quickly, while others will not. What governs the speed by which party attachments lose their strength in the absence of reinforcement?

As suggested above, a crucial factor affecting the durability of a behavior is the way the behavior was learned, or more precisely, the nature and extent of prior reinforcement for the behavior. A behavior should be most resistant to change if it has acquired its stength through irregular reinforcement over a long span of time.[12] It should be least resistant to change if it

---

12. This may explain the familiar observation that the party attachments of the middle-aged and the old are more durable than the attachments of the young (Converse 1976). They have simply talked about parties for a longer time than the young, whose susceptibility to partisan change is the simple effect of political inexperience. In fact, of the Japanese in the 1967 survey

has acquired its strength through regular reinforcement over a short span of time.

These relationships lead to a number of expectations about the probable durability of individual party attachments, given that individuals have experienced different histories of social reinforcement for their party attachments. If it is assumed that regular reinforcement for party attachments is likely to occur in social environments which are partisanly homogeneous, different patterns for individual histories of social reinforcement can be identified. The following section sets out a number of predictions about rates of change, points out how these predictions are linked to the components of learning theory, and compares them to the actual observed rates of change.

Prediction 1.

Rates of partisan change should be high for those who initially held a party attachment compatible with an early homogeneous environment, but now line in an environment that is hostile to that attachment. The rates should be high because these individuals as youths probably received regular reinforcement for their partisan behavior. This pattern of reinforcement should generate strong attachments, but attachments that are not especially durable if the social environment changes and becomes more hostile. This prediction is exactly opposite that which would follow if we hypothesized that the absence of cross-pressure in the initial environment would lead to stronger, and hence more stable, party attachments.

Findings. To test this prediction we need to compare rates of partisan change for individuals who grew up in a homogeneous environment, initially held a party attachment compatible with that environment, but who now live in an environment hostile to that attachment, with the rates of partisan change for individuals who are identical except that they grew up in a compatible environment that was less homogeneous. For Italy, the appropriate comparison is between the rate of partisan change for individuals located in four test groups with the rate of partisan change for individuals located in eight other control groups.[13] Making computations from the figures found in

who reported that they had once switched parties, virtually all said that they had done so when they were young, between the ages of 18 and 25.
13. Test groups for Italy: R.Hom to L.Het and R.Hom to L.Hom, for those with an initial attachment with a party of the right; L.Hom to R.Hom and L.Hom to R.Het, for those with an initial attachment with a party of the

Table 3, the rate for Italians in the test groups (7.3 percent) is slightly below the rate for those in the control groups (8.9 percent), and not higher, as we had predicted. However, the difference is small enough to also cast doubt on the conventional explanation. Unfortunately, the sample size for individuals in the test groups is so small (N = 41) that it is probably best to suspend judgment.

For Japan, when computations are made from the figures in Table 4, the appropriate comparison is between the rate of partisan change for individuals in a single test group and the rate of partisan change for individuals located in six other control groups.[14] Here, the rate for Japanese in the test groups (19.5 percent) was much higher than the rate for the control groups (8.3 percent), so the prediction was confirmed; again, however, the sample size for the test group is so small (raw N = 23) that final judgment is impossible.[15] This is unfortunate, since the individuals in the test groups have experienced the most drastic shifts in partisan environment and, hence, in patterns of reinforcement. According to current theory, a party attachment that is reinforced regularly when one is young should be more durable. The results here, although they are only suggestive, do not support such a view. Such party attachments may actually be less durable.

Discussion. If our hypothesis is correct, we might expect substantial change in the distribution of partisanship in countries undergoing rapid social change of the sort that breaks down subcultural barriers and puts individuals into more heterogeneous social environments. The Netherlands is an obvious example of such a country. Yet even in Italy, and to a lesser extent in Japan, there are still subcultural pockets that are partisanly homogeneous. Post-industrial change may eliminate these environments altogether.

---

left. Control groups for Italy: R.Het to L.Het, R.Het to L.Hom, Heter to L.Het, and Heter to L.Hom, for those with an initial attachment with a party of the right; L.Het to R.Het, L.Het to R.Hom, Heter to R.Het, and Heter to R.Hom., for those with an initial attachment with a party of the left.
14. Test group for Japan: R.Hom to L.Het, for those with an initial attachment with a party of the right. Control groups for Japan: R.Het to L.Het and Heter to L.Het, for those with an initial attachment with a party of the right; L.Het to R.Hom, L.Het to R.Het, Heter to R.Het, and Heter to R.Hom, for those with an initial attachment with a party of the left.
15. A raw N of 23 is about 1.2 percent of the entire sample, which has a raw N of 1,973. Of course the sampling error associated with any estimate of a proportion for such a small subsample will be quite large. With only 4 individuals of 23 switching, I did not feel that a chi-square test was appropriate because of small cell sizes.

Prediction 2

The rate of partisan change should be very high for individuals who were deviants as youths, but who live as adults in a social environment that is incompatible with such a deviant party attachment. For some unknown reason these individuals, as youths, managed to pick up party attachments that were different from those supported by their social environments. It is likely that there was little reinforcement for their partisan behavior, and their attachments were probably weak. Over time, if the partisan direction of these individuals' social environments does not change, their attachments should become steadily weaker and should eventually be abandoned altogether. This would happen because behaviors which cease to be reinforced should be extinguished.

Findings. The relevant comparison for testing this prediction is between the rate of change for deviants who remain in a hostile environment and the overall rate of change for all individuals. For Italy these deviants are found in eight test groups (N = 180) and for Japan in five test groups (raw N = 130).[16] The rate of change for individuals in the eight test groups in Italy was 15.0 percent, a figure much higher than the overall rate for Italians of 5.6 percent, so the prediction is confirmed for Italy. The comparable rates for Japan are 19.9 percent and 9.2 percent, so the prediction is confirmed for Japan also.

Discussion. The finding that deviants are more likely than others to abandon their party attachment is important because deviants, in societies where heterogeneous social environments predominate, are likely to be attached to small parties. Small parties will thus tend to lose supporters at a high rate, and just to survive must find ways of continuously replenishing their losses. Usually this can be accomplished only by maximizing short-term forces, by paying careful attention to the candidates they run and the issue positions they take. Like the small grocery competing against the large supermarket, they must offer a better product or service. If they do not, they will fail. The only other option can be suicidal—increased specialization and retreat into a homogeneous subcultural pocket that may well vanish.

---

16. Test groups for Italy: L.Hom to L.Hom, L.Hom to L.Het, L.Het to L.Hom, and L.Het to L.Het, for those with an initial attachment with a party on the right; R.Hom to R.Hom, R.Hom to R.Het, R.Het to R.Hom, and R.Het to R.Het, for those with an initial attachment with a party on the left. Test groups for Japan: L.Het to L.Het, for those with an initial attachment with a party on the right; R.Hom to R.Hom, R.Hom to R.Het, R.Het to R.Hom, and R.Het to R.Het, for those with an initial attachment with a party on the left.

Prediction 3

Those individuals who acquired a party attachment in a heterogeneous environment, or in an environment that was heterogeneous but unbalanced in a direction compatible with that attachment, should tend to be more stable than others, whatever the partisan characteristics of their adult social environment. This should be so because the attachments of these individuals were probably acquired under conditions of irregular and unpredictable reinforcement. Their attachments should be more durable than the attachments of others, particularly when as adults they are in social environments that are hostile to these attachments.

Findings. In both Italy and Japan the relevant comparisons are between the rates of partisanship change for individuals who grew up in either a heterogeneous or an unbalanced heterogeneous environment, and acquired a party attachment compatible with that environment, and the rates of change for individuals who acquired the same party attachment initially but happened to grow up in a favorable homogeneous or an unfavorable environment. The comparisons should be made so that the final environment is controlled. To accomplish this, for individuals who initially identified with a party on the right, look up the right-heterogeneous and heterogeneous columns of Tables 3 and 4 and compare the percentages in these two columns, row by row, with the percentages on either side. If the prediction is correct, these percentages should be lower than the percentages to either side. For individuals who initially identified with a party on the left, look up the left-heterogeneous and heterogeneous columns.

In Italy, comparisons are possible in six rows (see Table 3). In these six rows there are twenty possible pairwise comparisons, and, of these, thirteen show a lower percentage for individuals who grew up in a heterogeneous environment, or a heterogeneous but unbalanced environment. This result is in the predicted direction, but is not especially convincing. For Japan, comparisons are also possible in six rows (Table 4). In these rows there are fourteen possible pairwise comparisons, and, of these, thirteen show a lower percentage for individuals in the test groups. This result is much more convincing.

Discussion. The poorer result in Italy may be due to the much lower overall rate of partisan change in that country (5.6 percent) than in Japan (9.2 percent). There are simply fewer "switchers" in Italy than in Japan upon which to base estimates of partisan change, and since the differences in percentages in Italy are small, the comparisons will be more sensitive to sampling error. Still, the results are compatible with our theory for both countries. Party attachments acquired in heterogeneous but compatible environments appear to be more stable than those acquired in other sorts of environments.

Prediction 4

Whatever the partisan characteristics of the initial environment, the likelihood of defection should increase most dramatically when the partisan characteristics of the adult environment are unbalanced in a direction hostile to the initial attachment. This hypothesis is a straightforward application of learning theory: positive reinforcement should strengthen behavior and prolong it; negative reinforcement will tend to extinguish it. For those with party attachments, the likelihood of losing the attachment or switching to another party should depend upon the ratio of positive to negative reinforcement that they get for their partisan views, and this ratio should depend on the partisan characteristics of the adult environment. The ratio should be high when the adult environment is compatible with the initial attachment, and low when it is not. Only when the ratio is low will we ordinarily expect the party attachment to be lost. This reasoning, of course, is not incompatible with the finding (Campbell et al. 1964) that changes of party attachments due to personal reasons are for the most part caused by changes in social circumstances. Such changes might well alter substantially the ratio of positive to negative reinforcement. For example, an Italian woman who is attached to the DC, but who marries into a Communist family, may feel strong social pressures from this family to abandon her attachment. This reasoning, however, is not compatible with the notion that the effects of social influence are always additive. If this were true we would expect that the likelihood of defection from an initial attachment would increase in steady, incremental fashion as the partisan characteristics of the adult environment become more hostile.

Findings. We can examine the column totals in Tables 3 and 4 to determine whether the largest increases in the likelihood of defection are found between adult environments that are heterogeneous, but unbalanced in a hostile direction. A comparison of differences in percentages between adjacent column totals shows that this is the case for both Italy and Japan. The differences in percentages for Italy are 6.8 percent (initial attachment to a party on the right) and 6.5 percent (initial attachment to a party on the left). These are larger than the differences in percentages between any other adjacent column totals. The equivalent differences in percentages for Japan are 5.0 and 5.7 percent.

We can contrast this unambiguous result with the results from a test of the notion that the effects of social influence are always additive. If this is so, we would expect that the column totals will always be monotonic—that is, as the adult environment becomes more hostile to the initial attachment, the likelihood of defection should increase. It should be noted that this is a rather easy test, since we are not even requiring that the effects of changes in social environment upon defections be about equal, just that they be in the same direction. For Italy there are twelve possible pairwise comparisons, and of these, nine were in a direction consistent with the hypothesis. For Japan there were nine possible comparisons, and of these seven were in a direction consistent with the hypothesis. These results are ambiguous enough to cast some doubt on the hypothesis that social influence always has additive effects.

Discussion. It should not be surprising that a party attachment is most likely to be either abandoned or changed when the adult social environment is hostile to such an attachment. Such a finding is consistent with the view that party attachments are social identifications and are used by individuals to adjust to the politically relevant contingencies of their social environments. So long as one particular party attachment is as good as any other (i.e., gets as much positive reinforcement as another), there would be little advantage in changing. It is interesting, from this perspective, to note the single case where the effects of the adult social environment do seem to be steady and incremental—for individuals in Italy initially identifying with a party on the left. The leftist in Italy lives in a country which is the home of the Catholic Church and in which the Church is still the dominant cultural institution. It may be very difficult for individuals to resist such influence since, unless they are isolated to some extent, it will be an omnipresent part of their social environment. An Italian who is sympathetic to the left may still be asked by his priest why he was not at Sunday mass, or he may be warned that a vote for the Communists is a vote against his family and God. In Japan, however, there are no institutions with a cultural influence as great as that of the Catholic Church in Italy. The left is not so potent a threat to traditional cultural values, and nobody will sin by voting for the JSP.

Summary

There appears to be a rather close correspondence between relative rates of partisan change and the predictions about such rates that would follow from a straightforward application of learning theory. This is encouraging, since a single theory may now be capable of explaining how social environments can cause change in party attachments. Our theory can deal with some phenomena inadequately covered by earlier theories. With regard to the question of absolute rates of partisan change, however, the problem is much more difficult. For some categories of individuals--those, for example, who picked up an attachment in a homogeneous environment but as adults find themselves in an environment completely hostile to their initial attachment—we might expect that everyone would abandon their attachments. This didn't happen. The problem here is not so much with the theory but with the quality of the data and what can be done with them. Our method of classification of individuals into social environments can only hope to measure the most general features of individual learning histories. This makes it impossible to make predictions for individual cases, and may well account for the rather modest relationships discovered in some of our analyses. Of course, further research with better specification of contextual variables is required to test whether or not this suspicion is correct. There is also the problem of explaining the lower overall rate of partisan change for Italy (5.6 percent) than for Japan (9.2 percent). A plausible explanation would be differences in individual partisan environments, which seem to have been more stable for Italians. In Italy, 49.3 percent initially identifying with the right lived as adults in environments compatible with that attachment; the figure for those initially identifying with the left was 48.2 percent. For Japan, the corresponding figures are somewhat lower--44.0 and 35.6 percent. However, if we control for initial and final social environments by making comparisons of defection rates across the eighteen groups where this is possible (see Tables 3 and 4), the Italian rate is lower than the Japanese rate in seventeen cases. My own guess is that these differences in defection rates must surely be linked to the fact that in Italy the Communist Party is a serious contender for political power at the national level, whereas in Japan the Socialists and other parties on the left have not been especially credible contenders. A switch to the left in Italy has potentially "grave" consequences; a switch to the left in Japan, while not frivolous, can be a simple act of protest without any long-range consequences. Evidence from the 1968 Italian survey suggests that this is the correct interpretation. Of those interviewed (N = 2,500), 24.5 percent said that they would never vote for a party of the extreme left (either the PCI or the Italian Socialist Party of Proletarian Unity), and another 12.4 percent said that they would not vote for the PCI and some combination of other parties. In Japan, it is commonplace in newspaper election surveys to find that many who vote for the opposition do not actually wish to see those parties take the reins of power from the LDP.

Strength of Party Attachments

The strength of a party attachment, or the frequency/intensity with which individuals show their support for a party verbally, should depend directly on the extent to which such expressions of support are encouraged by others (or receive reinforcement) in the current social environment. Whenever such expressions of support are encouraged, attachments should be strengthened; whenever they are not, attachments should be weakened.

This hypothesis about what affects the strength of party attachments is somewhat different from the argument that was presented by Converse (1969). According to his view, party attachments should be strengthened over time as a function of experience with a political party. He labelled this the "learning" phenomenon. After he set out his hypothesis, a variety of evidence accumulated that seemed to support such a view. For example, there is generally a positive association between age (used as a measure of experience with a party) and strength of partisanship in those countries which have historically had a stable party system. Results of this type were found in Great Britain (Butler and Stokes 1971), the Netherlands (Jennings 1972), Norway (Campbell and Valen 1966), and the United States (Campbell et al. 1964). In countries where the party system has not been stable this association often does not exist, or is modified somewhat. This has occurred in India (Eldersveld 1973), Italy (Converse 1969), and Japan (Richardson 1975). For the United States, Converse (1976) has also analyzed cohort data and concluded that the mean strength of party identification for different age cohorts generally did increase over time, especially for the more stable period before 1965.

We might hypothesize, however, that such an increase is not due to "experience" so much as it is due to the impact of experience on social environments. As individuals progress through the life cycle their social environments tend to become more clearly defined and, hence, more stable. Reinforcement becomes more regular and predictable. Indeed progress through the life cycle generates opportunities to choose social environments. As Finifter (1974) has shown, most individuals will prefer a social environment where their partisan views are more regularly and predictably reinforced. For all of these reasons, progression through the life cycle is likely to mean a stronger party attachment. Older individuals are simply more likely to find themselves in a homogeneous, compatible environment.

We can test the hypothesis that the strength of party attachments depends on patterns of reinforcement in the current environment by looking at the proportions of strong to weak attachments in adult environments of varying compatibility and homogeneity/heterogeneity. There are at least three situations.

In one situation, when individuals are located within a social environment that is entirely hostile to their partisan views, these views will receive little if any reinforcement. Party attachments should be weak. If this situation continues, individuals should be more and more likely to abandon their attachments, and, for this reason, we would naturally anticipate finding fewer left identifiers in a right-homogeneous environment, and vice versa. This prediction has already been confirmed in Figure 1, which shows a clear relationship between the adult environment and the direction of party attachment (i.e., there are large differences between the total row percentages). However, we would further anticipate that those who do manage to retain their party attachments in such an environment must have had, at least initially, rather strong attachments. The guess is that they must have found reinforcement for their attachments in other ways, despite the hostility of their immediate social environment. For this reason the ratio of strong to weak identifiers in such social environments should be higher than would be the case if many of those who were initially attached only weakly had not fallen away.

In a second situation, when individuals are located within social environments which are only partially compatible with their partisan views, these views will receive only irregular and unpredictable reinforcement. Their attachments should be of moderate strength. Since conversions in such social environments should be limited in number, even for those with only weak attachments, the ratio of strong to weak identifiers should be fairly low.

A final possibility is when individuals are located within social environments that are wholly or almost wholly compatible with their partisan views. Regular reinforcement in such environments should lead to attachments which are strong. Conversions should again be limited in number, so that the ratio of strong to weak attachments should be quite high.

The resulting prediction is that a curvilinear relationship should exist between the adult environment and the strength of partisanship among identifiers: there should be a higher ratio of strong to weak identifiers in both favorable and hostile adult environments, as compared with more heterogeneous envrionments. The highest ratio should be found in favorable adult environments (homogeneous and compatible, or heterogeneous but unbalanced in a compatible direction), the next highest ratio in hostile environments

TABLE 5
Strength of Party Attachments
and the Partisan Characteristics
of the Adult Social Environment

A. Italy

Attachment with Party on Left[a]

	L.Hom	L.Het	Heter	R.Het	R.Hom
Strong[b]	46.1%	48.1%	34.5%	30.5%	35.7%
Weak[c]	53.9	51.9	65.5	69.5	64.3
Total	100.0%	100.0%	100.0%	100.0%	100.0%
	(76)	(295)	(171)	(200)	(14)

Attachment with Party on Right

	L.Hom	L.Het	Heter	R.Het	R.Hom
Strong	56.3%	39.7%	39.9%	44.3%	55.3%
Weak	43.8	60.3	61.1	55.8	44.7
Total	100.1%	100.0%	100.0%	100.1%	100.0%
	(16)	(156)	(386)	(524)	(47)

Notes:
    a. Attachment strength indicated by response to survey question: "Would you say that you feel very close to this party, more or less close, or not very close?"
    b. "very close"
    c. "more or less close" and "not very close"

B. Japan

Attachment with JSP[a]

	L.Het	Heter	R.Het	R.Hom
Strong[b]	23.5%	21.1%	12.7%	14.3%
Weak[c]	76.5	78.9	87.3	85.7
Total	100.0%	100.0%	100.0%	100.0%
	(146)	(175)	(84)	(14)

Attachment with LDP

	L.Het	Heter	R.Het	R.Hom
Strong	13.3%	13.9%	20.4%	16.8%
Weak	86.7	86.1	79.6	83.2
Total	100.0%	100.0%	100.0%	100.0%
	(119)	(255)	(242)	(50)

Notes:
    a. Attachment strength indicated by response to survey question: "How strongly do you support (chosen party)—very strongly, or just support it?"
    b. "very strongly"
    c. "just support"

(homogeneous, but not compatible), and the lowest ratio in heterogeneous environments, or in heterogeneous environments which are unbalanced in a hostile direction. Unfortunately, as noted above, we lack a direct measurement of strength (verbal intensity/frequency), and so must make do with the standard questionnaire item. Even so, the predictions do quite well, as can be seen in Table 5. Apparently, it is the partisan characteristics of the adult social environment that establish the patterns of reinforcement that affect the strength of party attachments.

Cross-National Variations in the Strength of Party Attachments: A Digression

A check on the generality of this hypothesis about the relationship between the homogeneity/heterogeneity of the adult social environment and the strength of party attachments is provided by an examination of national-level evidence. There are striking differences in the ratio between strong and weak identifiers among countries (see column F, Table 6). I hypothesize that these differences are explained by two factors: the patterns of social cleavage—whether they lead to social environments which are mostly homogeneous or heterogeneous--and the degree of party system fragmentation. Each of these factors should be causally important in shaping the nature of reinforcement that individuals receive for their partisan views. The relative homogeneity/heterogeneity of social environments determines the extent of regularity of social reinforcement for partisan views. Of course, "social environment" here refers not to the homogeneity or heterogeneity of the entire society, but rather to the likelihood of any individual being situated in an immediate environment that provides more or less regular reinforcement for the expression of particular partisan viewpoints. Indeed, to the extent that a country is split into identifiable and mutually exclusive groups (particularly if regionally based), the immediate social environments of individuals are more likely to be homogeneous (and therefore, provide regular reinforcement). Impressionistic evidence suggests that India, Italy, the Netherlands, Norway, and West Germany fall in this category.[17] Conversely,

___

17. Major social cleavages of political relevance in India include caste, language (Hindi and others) and religion (Hindu vs. Muslim). See Hardgrave (1975:109-76); see also Eldersveld and Ahmed (1978). In Italy social cleavages include religion (Catholic vs. nonpracticing) and social class. See Barnes (1971, 1974), Galli and Prandi (1970) and Sani (1974, 1975b, 1976). Cleavages in the Netherlands include religion (Catholic vs. Calvinist vs. Dutch

TABLE 6
Environmental Homogeneity/Heterogeneity, Party System
Fragmentation, and the Ratio of Strong to Weak Party Attachments

A. Example	B. Social Environments	C. Party System Fragmentation[a]		D. % Strong Attachment[b]	E. % Weak Attachment	F. Ratio (D/E)
India (1967)	homogeneous	low	.487	P	51	19	2.7
W. Germany (1972)	homogeneous	low	.614[c]	M	50	20	2.5
Norway (1965)	homogeneous	high	.691	P	36	32	1.1
Italy (1968) (1972)	homogeneous	high	.721	EP	33 23	50 49	0.7 0.5
Netherlands (1970)	homogeneous	high	.787	SM	18	25	0.7
G. Britain (1963) (1964) (1966)	heterogeneous	low	.512	T	32 43 43	57 47 38	0.6 0.9 1.1
U. States (1956) (1976)	heterogeneous	low	.483	T	35 24	39 39	0.9 0.6
Canada (1974)	heterogeneous	high	.574	T	27	39	0.7
France (1967)	heterogeneous	high	.620	P	22	46	0.5
Japan (1967)	heterogeneous	high	.645	P	11	47	0.2

Notes:
a. Decimals are the mean values for each country of Rae's index of fractionalization computed for elections held from 1945-1973 (for France, the Fifth Republic, 1958-1973): a larger decimal means a greater degree of fractionalization; figures reported in Giovanni Sartori (1976:313). Capital letters are codes for Sartori's party system typology: EP = extreme (format) polarized (mechanics); SM = segmented (format) moderate (mechanics); M = moderate pluralism; T = two-party; P = predominant.
b. Base upon which percentages were figured includes the entire sample, and not just those with party attachments.
c. The Rae index for West Germany probably exaggerates the extent of party system fragmentation since it distinguishes between the CDU and the CSU.

Sources:
India (1967): Eldersveld, 1973.
West Germany (1972): computed from ICPSR study; principal investigators Manfred Berger, Wolfgang Bibowski, Max Kaase, Pieter Roth, Uwe Schleth, and Rudolf Wildenmann.
Norway (1965): computed from ICPSR study; principal investigator Henry Valen.
Italy (1968): computed from data furnished by Samuel Barnes.
(1972): computed from the Barnes-Sani 1972 study.
Netherlands (1970): computed from ICPSR study; principal investigators Felix Heunks, M. Kent Jennings, Warren E. Miller, Philip C. Stouthard, and Jacques Thomassen.
Great Britain (1963, 1964, 1966): computed from ICPSR studies; principal investigators David Butler and Donald Stokes.
United States (1956, 1976): computed from the national election study series, Center for Political Studies, University of Michigan.
Canada (1974): computed from ICPSR study; principal investigators Harold Clarke, Jane Jenson, Lawrence Leduc, and Jon Pammett.
France (1967): computed from ICPSR study; principal investigators Philip E. Converse, Georges Dupeux, and Roy Pierce.
Japan (1967): computed from ICPSR study; principal investigators Akira Kubota and Robert E. Ward.

in countries where basic social cleavages are more cross-cutting or diffuse (and less regionally based), chances are higher that an individual's immediate social environment will be less homogeneous and provide less regular reinforcement. The United States, France, Canada, and Japan seem to fall into this category. Great Britain seems to be intermediate between these two categories.[18] An additional factor is the party system: it seems clear that when there are more parties, with fewer supporters for each, reinforcement

Reformed) and social class. See Lijphart (1974) and Lorwin (1971). In the late 1960's and 1970's the "pillars" of Dutch society began to fall down and there is now an umbrella Christian Democratic Party which was formed from the merger of the formerly hostile KVP, ARP, and CHU. In Norway important social cleavages include urban vs. rural, tradition vs. modernism (e.g., controversies over issues such as the role of religion in education and the use of alcohol), social class, and language. See Valen and Katz (1964) and Eckstein (1966). In West Germany there are divisions based on religion (Catholic vs. Protestant vs. secular) and social class. The society is now becoming more heterogeneous (Baker, Dalton, and Hildebrandt, 1975). Also see the article by Urwin (1974).

18. In the United States, regional and ethnic cleavages have dominated politics. Currently, the major regional cleavage is between North and South, but this seems to be declining in importance. It may be replaced by one between states with stagnant economies (central and northeast) and states with dynamic economies (mountain, southwest, pacific). The major ethnic cleavage is between black and white and remains highly salient. See the article by Walter D. Burnham (1974). For the most part, however, social environments in the United States are marked by great heterogeneity. In France the major social cleavages are religion (Catholic vs. anti-clerical) and social class (bourgeoisie vs. working class), but are far less sharp than in Italy. There is also a center vs. periphery cleavage because of the fact that Paris, more so than the principal cities of other countries, dominates the cultural and political life of the nation. Another cleavage of growing importance in France is that between individuals who hold materialist values and those who hold what are called "post-industrial" or "post-materialist" values; see Ingelhart (1977). The only social cleavage of long-standing importance in Canada is language—between English-speaking provinces and French-speaking Quebec; however, regional strains have always existed between the populous provinces of Quebec and Ontario and the resource-rich western provinces. See Schwartz (1974). Japan is a country that, happily or not, lacks any really major social cleavages. Class identification is unusually low. The most politically salient division is between those who are organized into leftist unions (Sōhyō and Dōmei) and those who are not; there is also a major religious sect, the Sōkagakkai, whose members provide the bulk of the support for the Clean Government Party (CGP), the third-largest parliamentary party. Public employees also form a distinct group. See Nakane (1970) and Ward (1960). (In Great Britain the dominant social cleavage is social class; see Butler and Stokes 1971. This cleavage, however, seems to be of declining political significance.)

for any one should be less regular. One way of measuring the degree of party system fragmentation is to use Rae's index of fractionalization in combination with Sartori's party system typology (Sartori 1976:310-11, 313). If this is done, countries such as India, West Germany, Great Britain, and the United States seem to have a low degree of party system fragmentation. Countries such as Norway, Italy, the Netherlands, France, and Japan seem to have a high degree of party system fragmentation. Canada seems to be intermediate. These classifications are all displayed in Table 6.

Our predictions are well confirmed by the cross-national data. At one extreme, in the countries with homogeneous social environments and a low degree of party system fragmentation (India and West Germany), the ratio of strong to weak identifiers is very high. At the other extreme, in the countries with heterogeneous social environments and a high degree of party system fragmentation (France and Japan), the ratio of strong to weak identifiers is very low. In countries with homogeneous social environments and a high degree of party system fragmentation (Italy and the Netherlands), the ratio of strong to weak identifiers is also low, but not quite so low as for France and Japan. The country of Norway seems to be intermediate.[19] Social environments are homogeneous, but the party system is not quite so fragmented as for Italy and the Netherlands. In countries like Great Britain and the United States, the heterogeneity of social environments is apparently balanced by what are basically two-party systems, and strong and weak identifiers are found in more nearly equal numbers. The ratios for Great Britain are probably higher because of the homogeneity introduced by the class division (see Butler and Stokes 1971:71-94). Canada seems to be intermediate. Like the United States, social environments are heterogeneous, but unlike the United States, the party system is more fragmented. The ratio for Canada is low, and approaches the ratios for France and Japan.

We might suggest that of these two factors, party system fragmentation seems to be somewhat more important. Fragmentation makes a great deal of difference for countries where social environments are homogeneous; it makes some difference where they are heterogeneous. On the other hand, the impact of social heterogeneity appears to be somewhat more uniform, regardless of the degree of party system fragmentation.

---

19. Norway is difficult to classify. It has a predominant party system, like that of India, but the degree of party system fragmentation, as is suggested by the .691 Rae Index, would seem to place it in the "high" category in terms of fragmentation.

One final note: the Japanese ratio (0.2) appears remarkably low even given its classification as a country with heterogeneous social environments and high party system fragmentation. A highly plausible explanation is the institutional factor, Japan's peculiar electoral system, examined in detail by Thomas Rochon in this volume. We can infer from his analysis that if Japan had a single-member constituency system, or more particularly a proportional representation system, its ratio of strong to weak identifiers would be considerably higher. The same may be true, to a lesser extent, of France. Under the electoral system of the Fifth Republic, where run-off elections are possible, parties commonly form coalitions to enter and withdraw candidates at both the first and the second ballots. Combined with the penchant of French parties for changing their names, things can get quite confusing. Attachments should weaken under such circumstances.

Although this cross-national analysis might require refinement and a larger sample of countries to be completely convincing, it does support our hypothesis that the degree of homogeneity/heterogeneity of the immediate social environment does have an important impact on the strength of an individual's party attachment. Other factors, such as the degree of party system fragmentation, and the electoral system, may have even more powerful effects. These results were obtained, however, using only the standard questionnaire items. It is hoped that better results will be obtained when strength is measured as the frequency/intensity of partisan behavior in everyday social environments.

Conclusion

Much of the research to date on the causes underlying the stability and strength of party attachments has not been guided by a theory which is capable of explaining the dynamics of individual behavior. We have suggested that for social behaviors like party attachments, whose stability and strength depend upon patterns of reinforcement from a social environment, only learning theory is likely to be successful in this task. The application of this theory, however, compels us to abandon the popular conceptualization of party attachments as "attitudes," the presence of which can only be inferred, and think instead of party attachments as verbal behavior. This theory also compels us to distinguish between two separate dimensions of party attachments: their strength, the frequency/intensity with which partisan verbal behavior is performed, and their durability, the ability of the attachment to persist in the absence of social reinforcement.

A secondary analysis of survey data from Italy and Japan points to the importance of the partisan homogeneity/heterogeneity of the social environments of individuals, both when they are youths and when they are adults, in affecting the durability of party attachments. The strength of party attachments, on the other hand, seems to depend most upon the adult social environment. It is important to note that these conclusions are based on data which were collected more than a decade ago. The findings are not unimportant, however, to an understanding of the nature and direction of developments which have occurred in party politics in both Italy and Japan since then, or for that matter, to an understanding of possible future developments.

The social changes that have accompanied the advance of post-industrial society have tended, in both countries, to eliminate social environments that are partisanly homogeneous. These changes have probably progressed somewhat further in Japan than in Italy, due to the somewhat faster rate of economic growth in Japan, and also to the absence there of any institution, like the Catholic Church, that is a basis of cultural cleavage and, hence, of partisan isolation. Nonetheless, for both countries we could have predicted, more than a decade ago, that the proportion of independents or unattached individuals would grow, due partly to failures of partisanship transmission and the difficulties of picking up attachments in heterogeneous environments, but also due to individuals who had acquired their attachments in an homogeneous environment abandoning their attachments as their social environment became more hostile.

We could have predicted a substantial decline in the levels of support for both the DC and the LDP, due for the most part to losses that would be incurred from the deaths of older supporters and our realization that these parties were unlikely to soon devise an effective strategy for attracting the young as supporters. This prediction, however, would have had to be qualified.

To a large extent, we also would have expected that the small parties in Italy and Japan, as individual entities and because of their small size, would face a future even more hazardous than that of large parties like the DC and the LDP. Those small parties which competed in heterogeneous environments would face serious problems in retaining their supporters. Those who were attached to these parties would be isolated, would receive little reinforcement for their partisan views, and, as a consequence, would tend to hold weak attachments. With little or no reinforcement, they would be much more likely than the supporters of large parties to eventually abandon their attachments.

The postwar period, at least in Italy, has confirmed this scenario. It is true that small parties in Italy are protected by the system of proportional representation. Nonetheless, the support for all of the Italian small parties (Italian Socialist Party of Proletarian Unity, Social Democrats, Republicans, Liberals, and Monarchists) has seemed to be in perpetual decline, and has been reversed only temporarily as a result of beneficial short-term forces. Indeed, several parties--the Italian Socialist Party of Proletarian Unity, an offshoot of the Social Democrats, and the Monarchists—did lose their identities by merging with other parties. The only small party in Italy that has escaped this pattern is the Italian Social Movement, which has depended more than any other small party in Italy on supporters located in homogeneously partisan environments.

The postwar experience of small parties in Japan has been somewhat different. In Japan small parties are protected by the electoral system of multi-member districts. Unlike Italy, support for these parties has been more stable over the postwar period. The reason is probably the importance of candidates, as compared to parties, in Japanese elections. The Democratic Socialist, Clean Government, and Communist parties have been able to sustain their vote totals by running attractive candidates. The Clean Government and Communist parties have also invested heavily in organizational efforts at the grass-roots level. Nonetheless, there are indications that the small parties in Japan are not immune to the social environmental forces that erode attachments to small parties. The Japan Socialist Party, once fairly large, has steadily lost ground, and, like the Republicans in the United States, is in the precarious position of losing its "large" party status. The Clean Government Party suffered a reversal in 1972, and in the future may be driven into a subcultural pocket. Certainly the survival of such splinter parties as the New Liberal Club and the Socialist People's League is doubtful.

The futures of the DC and the LDP, as a result of the inevitable problems that will be faced by their smaller competitors, seems somewhat brighter than we might have expected based upon projections from previous trends. Both the DC and the LDP will benefit from their sheer size as post-industrial change continues to eliminate homogeneous social environments and put individuals into situations where they are exposed to conflicting partisan views. The future of the DC, as a large party in a society where this change still has some way to go, seems somewhat less secure than the future of the LDP, which has the additional advantages of being somewhat larger and of benefiting from an electoral system that does not translate votes directly into seats.

Appendix

Italy: Coding of Initial Environment

	Father's Party	Church School	Occupation	Region	Coded Environment	N
1.	Left	Yes	Middle	Left	Heter	1
2.	None	Yes	Middle	Left	R.Het	3
3.	Right	Yes	Middle	Left	R.Het	6
4.	Left	No	Middle	Left	L.Het	13
5.	None	No	Middle	Left	Heter	5
6.	Right	No	Middle	Left	R.Het	44
7.	Left	Yes	Working	Left	L.Het	2
8.	None	Yes	Working	Left	L.Het	2
9.	Right	Yes	Working	Left	Heter	1
10.	Left	No	Working	Left	L.Hom	13
11.	None	No	Working	Left	L.Hom	11
12.	Right	No	Working	Left	L.Het	67
13.	Left	Yes	Farm	Left	L.Het	0
14.	None	Yes	Farm	Left	Heter	1
15.	Right	Yes	Farm	Left	R.Het	6
16.	Left	No	Farm	Left	L.Hom	31
17.	None	No	Farm	Left	L.Hom	17
18.	Right	No	Farm	Left	Heter	227
19.	Left	Yes	None	Left	L.Het	0
20.	None	Yes	None	Left	Heter	0
21.	Right	Yes	None	Left	R.Het	0
22.	Left	No	None	Left	L.Hom	0
23.	None	No	None	Left	L.Hom	1
24.	Right	No	None	Left	Heter	11
25.	Left	Yes	Middle	Right	R.Het	2
26.	None	Yes	Middle	Right	R.Hom	10
27.	Right	Yes	Middle	Right	R.Hom	18
28.	Left	No	Middle	Right	R.Het	18
29.	None	No	Middle	Right	R.Hom	62
30.	Right	No	Middle	Right	R.Hom	141
31.	Left	Yes	Working	Right	Heter	0
32.	None	Yes	Working	Right	R.Het	1
33.	Right	Yes	Working	Right	R.Het	5
34.	Left	No	Working	Right	L.Het	27
35.	None	No	Working	Right	Heter	31
36.	Right	No	Working	Right	R.Het	144
37.	Left	Yes	Farm	Right	R.Het	0
38.	None	Yes	Farm	Right	R.Hom	1
39.	Right	Yes	Farm	Right	R.Hom	9

	Father's Party	Church School	Occupation	Region	Coded Environment	N
40.	Left	No	Farm	Right	Heter	25
41.	None	No	Farm	Right	R.Hom	93
42.	Right	No	Farm	Right	R.Hom	356
43.	Left	Yes	None	Right	R.Het	0
44.	None	Yes	None	Right	R.Hom	0
45.	Right	Yes	None	Right	R.Hom	5
46.	Left	No	None	Right	Heter	3
47.	None	No	None	Right	R.Hom	2
48.	Right	No	None	Right	R.Hom	26
49.	Left	Yes	Middle	Heter	R.Het	7
50.	None	Yes	Middle	Heter	R.Het	5
51.	Right	Yes	Middle	Heter	R.Het	31
52.	Left	No	Middle	Heter	Heter	32
53.	None	No	Middle	Heter	R.Het	78
54.	Right	No	Middle	Heter	R.Het	176
55.	Left	Yes	Working	Heter	L.Het	7
56.	None	Yes	Working	Heter	Heter	1
57.	Right	Yes	Working	Heter	R.Het	13
58.	Left	No	Working	Heter	L.Het	41
59.	None	No	Working	Heter	L.Het	24
60.	Right	No	Working	Heter	Heter	230
61.	Left	Yes	Farm	Heter	Heter	2
62.	None	Yes	Farm	Heter	R.Het	5
63.	Right	Yes	Farm	Heter	R.Het	12
64.	Left	No	Farm	Heter	L.Het	34
65.	None	No	Farm	Heter	Heter	49
66.	Right	No	Farm	Heter	R.Het	288
67.	Left	Yes	None	Heter	Heter	0
68.	None	Yes	None	Heter	R.Het	1
69.	Right	Yes	None	Heter	R.Het	4
70.	Left	No	None	Heter	L.Het	0
71.	None	No	None	Heter	Heter	2
72.	Right	No	None	Heter	R.Het	17

Coding:
  Father's Party: **Left:** PCI, PSI, and other Socialist, PRI; **Right:** DC, Catholic, Populist, Democratic, PLI, Monarchists, Fascist; **None:** no party, can't recall, no response.
  Church School: **Yes:** church school, church school and public school; **No:** public school, private, other, don't know, ought not to answer, no.
  Occupation: **Middle:** middle-class occupation; **Working:** working-class occupation; **Farm:** farmer; **None:** can't remember, no response.
  Region: Individuals who were older than 17 years of age in 1948: from South or Catholic Northeast, **Right;** from Red Belt provinces, **Left;** from all other parts of Italy, **Heter.** Individuals who were younger than 17 years of age in 1948: from Catholic Northeast, **Right;** from Red Belt provinces, **Left;** from all other parts of Italy, **Heter.**

Italy: Coding of Final Environment

	Union	Church Attendance	Class	Region	Coded Environment	N
1.	Cath	High	Working	Left	R.Het	3
2.	Left	High	Working	Left	L.Het	15
3.	Other	High	Working	Left	L.Het	168
4.	Cath	Low	Working	Left	Heter	1
5.	Left	Low	Working	Left	L.Hom	20
6.	Other	Low	Working	Left	L.Hom	102
7.	Cath	High	Middle	Left	R.Het	2
8.	Left	High	Middle	Left	Heter	2
9.	Other	High	Middle	Left	R.Het	80
10.	Cath	Low	Middle	Left	L.Het	2
11.	Left	Low	Middle	Left	L.Het	4
12.	Other	Low	Middle	Left	Heter	37
13.	Cath	High	Other	Left	R.Het	1
14.	Left	High	Other	Left	L.Het	1
15.	Other	High	Other	Left	Heter	11
16.	Cath	Low	Other	Left	Heter	0
17.	Left	Low	Other	Left	L.Hom	2
18.	Other	Low	Other	Left	L.Hom	5
19.	Cath	High	Working	Right	R.Hom	8
20.	Left	High	Working	Right	Heter	6
21.	Other	High	Working	Right	R.Het	157
22.	Cath	Low	Working	Right	R.Het	2
23.	Left	Low	Working	Right	L.Het	9
24.	Other	Low	Working	Right	Heter	33
25.	Cath	High	Middle	Right	R.Hom	5
26.	Left	High	Middle	Right	R.Het	1
27.	Other	High	Middle	Right	R.Hom	49
28.	Cath	Low	Middle	Right	R.Hom	1
29.	Left	Low	Middle	Right	R.Het	0
30.	Other	Low	Middle	Right	R.Hom	15
31.	Cath	High	Other	Right	R.Hom	1
32.	Left	High	Other	Right	R.Het	0
33.	Other	High	Other	Right	R.Hom	3
34.	Cath	Low	Other	Right	R.Hom	0
35.	Left	Low	Other	Right	L.Het	0
36.	Other	Low	Other	Right	Heter	0
37.	Cath	High	Working	Heter	R.Het	23
38.	Left	High	Working	Heter	Heter	13
39.	Other	High	Working	Heter	Heter	630
40.	Cath	Low	Working	Heter	R.Het	11
41.	Left	Low	Working	Heter	L.Het	46
42.	Other	Low	Working	Heter	L.Het	359
43.	Cath	High	Middle	Heter	R.Het	14
44.	Left	High	Middle	Heter	R.Het	10
45.	Other	High	Middle	Heter	R.Het	449
46.	Cath	Low	Middle	Heter	R.Het	5

	Union	Church Attendance	Class	Region	Coded Environment	N
47.	Left	Low	Middle	Heter	Heter	6
48.	Other	Low	Middle	Heter	R.Het	145
49.	Cath	High	Other	Heter	R.Het	0
50.	Left	High	Other	Heter	Heter	0
51.	Other	High	Other	Heter	R.Het	26
52.	Cath	Low	Other	Heter	R.Het	0
53.	Left	Low	Other	Heter	L.Het	0
54.	Other	Low	Other	Heter	L.Het	17

Coding:
    Union: **Cath:** Catholic union (CISL); **Left:** leftist union (CGIL); **Other:** non-affiliated union, not a union member, no response, not classifiable.
    Church Attendance: **High:** at least once a week, often during the year; **Low:** sometimes, rarely, never, no answer.
    Class: **Working:** working class; **Middle:** middle class; **Other:** other, no answer.
    Region: **Left:** individuals living in Red Belt provinces; **Right:** individuals living in Catholic Northeast; **Heter:** individuals living in places other than Red Belt or Catholic Northeast.

Japan: Coding of Initial Environment

	Father's Party	Class	Occupation	Location	Coded Environment	Raw N	Weighted N
1.	Right	Middle	Blue	Rural	R.Het	6	67
2.	Left	Middle	Blue	Rural	Heter	1	10
3.	None	Middle	Blue	Rural	R.Het	4	40
4.	Right	Other	Blue	Rural	R.Het	13	138
5.	Left	Other	Blue	Rural	L.Het	11	134
6.	None	Other	Blue	Rural	Heter	76	821
7.	Right	Middle	Other	Rural	R.Hom	98	1042
8.	Left	Middle	Other	Rural	L.Het	6	57
9.	None	Middle	Other	Rural	R.Hom	71	739
10.	Right	Other	Other	Rural	R.Hom	220	2393
11.	Left	Other	Other	Rural	L.Het	52	550
12.	None	Other	Other	Rural	R.Het	645	6758
13.	Right	Middle	Blue	Other	R.Het	9	90
14.	Left	Middle	Blue	Other	L.Het	1	22
15.	None	Middle	Blue	Other	Heter	8	80

	Father's Party	Class	Occupation	Location	Coded Environment	Raw N	Weighted N
16.	Right	Other	Blue	Other	R.Het	22	217
17.	Left	Other	Blue	Other	L.Het	17	194
18.	None	Other	Blue	Other	L.Het	66	719
19.	Right	Middle	Other	Other	R.Het	75	779
20.	Left	Middle	Other	Other	L.Het	7	78
21.	None	Middle	Other	Other	R.Het	73	744
22.	Right	Other	Other	Other	R.Het	122	1460
23.	Left	Other	Other	Other	L.Het	52	579
24.	None	Other	Other	Other	Heter	318	3336

Coding:
    Father's Party: **Right:** identified with LDP or pre-war conservative party; **Left:** identified with JSP, DSP, CGP, JCP, or pre-war progressive party; **None:** other identification, none, can't recall.
    Class: **Middle:** middle class; **Other:** working class, no response, other.
    Occupation: **Blue:** blue collar occupation in manufacturing, transportation, communications; **Other:** any other occupation, can't recall, no response.
    Location: **Rural:** identified place where respondent grew up as rural; **Other:** identified place where respondent grew up as small city, large city, and all other, can't recall, no response.

Japan: Coding of Final Environment

	District	Union	Class	Occupation	Coded Environment	Raw N	Weighted N
1.	LDP	Yes	Middle	Farm	R.Het	0	0
2.	Heter	Yes	Middle	Farm	Heter	1	10
3.	LDP	No	Middle	Farm	R.Hom	8	104
4.	Heter	No	Middle	Farm	R.Het	14	145
5.	LDP	Yes	Working	Farm	Heter	0	0
6.	Heter	Yes	Working	Farm	Heter	5	57
7.	LDP	No	Working	Farm	R.Hom	102	1059
8.	Heter	No	Working	Farm	R.Het	295	3098
9.	LDP	Yes	Middle	Blue	Heter	0	0
10.	Heter	Yes	Middle	Blue	L.Het	1	10
11.	LDP	No	Middle	Blue	R.Het	2	20
12.	Heter	No	Middle	Blue	Heter	5	50
13.	LDP	Yes	Working	Blue	L.Het	9	90
14.	Heter	Yes	Working	Blue	L.Het	33	346
15.	LDP	No	Working	Blue	Heter	59	614
16.	Heter	No	Working	Blue	L.Het	381	4113

	District	Union	Class	Occupation	Coded Environment	Raw N	Weighted N
17.	LDP	Yes	Middle	Other	R.Het	1	10
18.	Heter	Yes	Middle	Other	Heter	2	20
19.	LDP	No	Middle	Other	R.Het	12	120
20.	Heter	No	Middle	Other	R.Het	111	1196
21.	LDP	Yes	Working	Other	Heter	3	30
22.	Heter	Yes	Working	Other	L.Het	57	599
23.	LDP	No	Working	Other	R.Het	126	1266
24.	Heter	No	Working	Other	Heter	746	8090

Coding:
- District: **LDP:** LDP obtained 65% or more of the vote in 1967 election; **Heter:** all other districts.
- Union: **Yes:** member of family belongs to Sōhyō, Dōmei, or other union on left; **No:** member belongs to another union, no family member belongs to union, doesn't know, no response.
- Class: **Middle:** claims middle-class identification; **Working:** claims working-class identification, does not claim class identification, doesn't know, no response.
- Occupation: **Farm:** head of household is a farmer, head of household engages part time in agricultural occupation; **Blue:** head of household has occupation in manufacturing, transportation, communications; **Other:** head of household has another occupation, unemployed, doesn't know, no response.

Partisanship Strength Questions

Netherlands (1971): (If respondent names a party in ref. no. 145) Some people are strongly convinced adherents of their party. Others are not so strongly convinced adherents. Do you belong to the strongly convinced adherents of your party or not?

West Germany (1972): (If respondent leans toward a party) Taken altogether, how strongly or weakly do you lean towards this party: very strongly, fairly strongly (coded as **Strong**); moderately, fairly weakly, very weakly (coded as **Weak**)?

Canada (1974): How strongly do you feel (about party mentioned in Q.30A): very strongly (coded as **Strong**); fairly strongly, or not very strongly (coded as **Weak**)?

Norway (1965): (If respondent is party supporter) Do you consider yourself to be a strongly convinced supporter of your party, or are you not particularly strongly convinced?

Italy (1968): Would you say that you feel very close to this party (coded as **Strong**); more or less close, or not very close (coded as **Weak**)?

Japan (1967): (If respondent accepts party affiliation) How strongly do you support (chosen party)--very strongly, or just support it?

United States (1956 & 1978): (If respondent is coded, either a Democrat or a Republican) Would you call yourself a strong Republican or a not very strong Republican; or would you call yourself a strong Democrat or a not very strong Democrat?

France (1967): Do you feel that you are very close to this party (coded as **Strong**); fairly close, or not very close (coded as **Weak**)?

Britain (1963, 1964, & 1966): (If respondent accepts party affiliation) Well how strongly (chosen party) do you feel: very strongly (coded as **Strong**); fairly strongly, or not very strongly (coded as **Weak**)?

India (1967): Is your preference for this party very strong or not very strong?

References

Alexander, R. D. 1975. The search for a general theory of behavior. Behavioral Science, 20:77-100.

Allinson, G. D. 1975. Japanese urbanism: Industry and politics in Kariya, 1872-1972. Berkeley: University of California Press.

Baker, K. L., R. J. Dalton, and K. Hildebrandt. 1975. Political affiliations: Transition in the bases of German partisanship. Paper presented at the Workshop on Empirical and Theoretical Analysis of Party Systems, ECPR Joint Sessions, London, April 7-12, 1975.

Barnes, S. H. 1971. Left, right and the Italian voter. Comparative Political Studies, 4:156-76.

_____. 1974. Italy: religion and class in electoral behavior. In Richard Rose (ed.), Electoral behavior: A comparative handbook. New York: The Free Press, 171-226.

Berelson, B. R., P. F. Lazarsfeld, and W. N. McPhee. 1954. Voting. Chicago: University of Chicago Press.

Bitterman, M. E. 1975. The comparative analysis of learning. Science, 188:699-709.

Burnham, W. D. 1974. The United States: The politics of heterogeneity. In Richard Rose (ed.), Electoral behavior: A comparative handbook. New York: The Free Press, 653-725.

Butler, D., and D. E. Stokes. 1971. Political change in Britain. New York: St. Martin's Press.

Campbell, A., P. E. Converse, W. E. Miller, and D. E. Stokes. 1964. The American voter: An abridgement. New York: John Wiley & Sons.

Campbell, A., and H. Valen. 1966. Party identification in Norway and the United States. In A. Campbell, P. E. Converse, W. E. Miller, and D. E. Stokes (eds.), Elections and the political order. New York: John Wiley & Sons, 245-68.

Campbell, B. 1977. Change in the southern electorate. American Journal of Political Science, 21:37-64.

Converse, P. E. 1969. Of time and partisan stability. Comparative Political Studies, 2:139-71.

_____. 1976. The dynamics of party support. Beverly Hills: Sage.

Converse, P. E., and G. Dupeux. 1962. Politicization of the electorate in France and the United States. Public Opinion Quarterly, 26:1-23.

Curtis, G. L. 1971. Election campaigning Japanese style. New York: Columbia University Press.

Dennis, J., and D. J. McCrone. 1970. Preadult development of political party identification in Western democracies. Comparative Political Studies, 3:243-63.

Easton, D., and J. Dennis. 1969. Children in the political system. New York: McGraw-Hill.

Eckstein, H. 1966. Division and cohesion in democracy: A study of Norway. Princeton: Princeton University Press.

Eldersveld, S. J. 1973. Party identification in India in comparative perspective. Comparative Political Studies, 6:271-95.

Eldersveld, S. J., and B. Ahmed. 1978. Citizens and politics: Mass political behavior in India. Chicago: University of Chicago Press.

Finifter, A. W. 1974. The friendship group as a protective environment for political deviants. American Political Science Review, 68:607-625.

Flanagan, S. C. 1968. Voting behavior in Japan. Comparative Political Studies, 1:391-411.

_____. 1971. The Japanese party system in transition. Comparative Politics, 3:231-253.

Flanagan, S. C., and B. M. Richardson. 1977. Japanese electoral behavior: Social cleavages, social networks and partisanship. Beverly Hills: Sage.

_____. 1980. Political disaffection and political stability: A comparison of Japanese and Western findings. In Richard F. Tomasson (ed.), Comparative social research, Vol. III, Greenwich, Connecticut: JAI Press.

Galli, G., and A. Prandi. 1970. Patterns of political participation in Italy. New Haven: Yale University Press.

Hardgrave, R. L., Jr. 1975. India: Government and politics in a developing nation, 2nd ed. New York: Harcourt Brace Jovanovich.

Inglehart, R. 1977. The silent revolution: Changing values and political styles among Western publics. Princeton: Princeton University Press.

Jennings, M. K. 1972. Partisan commitment and electoral behavior in the Netherlands. Unpublished paper.

Jennings, M. K., and R. G. Niemi. n.d. The consequences of conjugal agreement patterns. Unpublished paper coauthored with Kenneth P. Langton.

Kubota, A., and R. E. Ward. 1970. Family influence and political socialization in Japan: Some preliminary findings in comparative perspective. Comparative Political Studies, 3:140-75.

Lazarsfeld, P., B. Berelson, and H. Gaudet. 1948. The people's choice. New York: Columbia University Press.

Lijphart, A. 1974. The Netherlands: Continuity and change in voting behavior. In Richard Rose (ed.), Electoral behavior: A comparative handbook. New York: The Free Press, 227-70.

Lorwin, V. R. 1971. Segmented pluralism: Ideological cleavages and political cohesion in the smaller European democracies. Comparative Politics, 3:141-75.

Miller, A. H., W. E. Miller, A. S. Raine, and T. A. Brown. 1976. A majority party in disarray: Political polarization in the 1972 election. American Political Science Review, 70:753-778.

Miller, W. E. 1956. One party politics and the voter. <u>American Political Science Review,</u> 50:707-725.

Nakane, C. 1970. <u>Japanese society.</u> Berkeley: University of California Press.

Nie, N., S. Verba, and J. Kim. 1974. Political participation and the life cycle. <u>Comparative Politics,</u> 6:319-340.

Nie, N. H., S. Verba, and J. R. Petrocik. 1976. <u>The changing American voter.</u> Cambridge: Harvard University Press.

Putnam, R. 1966. Political attitudes and the local community. <u>American Political Science Review,</u> 60:640-54.

Richardson, B. M. 1975. Party loyalties and party saliency in Japan. <u>Comparative Political Studies,</u> 8:32-57.

_____. 1977. Stability and change in Japanese voting behavior, 1958-1972. <u>Journal of Asian Studies,</u> 36: 675-93.

Sani, G. 1974. Determinants of party preference in Italy: Towards the integration of complementary models. <u>American Journal of Political Science,</u> 18:315-29.

_____. 1975a. Mass level response to party strategy: The Italian electorate and the communist party. In Donald L. Blackmer and Sidney Tarrow (eds.), <u>Communism in Italy and France,</u> Princeton: Princeton University Press, 456-503.

_____. 1975b. Secular trends and party realignments in Italy. Paper delivered at the meeting of the American Political Science Association, San Francisco, September 1975.

_____. 1976. Political traditions as contextual variables: Partisanship in Italy. <u>American Journal of Political Science,</u> 20:375-406.

Sani, G., and S. Barnes. 1972. Partisan change and the Italian voter: Some clues from the 1972 election. Paper delivered at the meeting of the International Political Science Association, Montreal, August 1973.

Sartori, Giovanni. 1976. <u>Parties and party systems: A framework for analysis.</u> New York: Cambridge University Press.

Schwartz, Mildred A. 1974. Canadian voting behavior. In Richard Rose (ed.), <u>Electoral behavior: A comparative handbook.</u> New York: The Free Press, 543-617.

Skinner, B. F. 1974. <u>About behaviorism.</u> New York: Alfred A. Knopf.

Skinner, B. F., and C. B. Ferster. 1957. Schedules of reinforcement. New York: Appleton-Crofts.

Strate, J. 1975. Alternative approaches to the understanding of a complex voter: The case of Japan. Unpublished paper.

Urwin, D. 1974. Germany: Continuity and change in electoral politics. In Richard Rose (ed.), Electoral behavior: A comparative handbook. New York: The Free Press, 109-170.

Valen, H., and D. Katz. 1964. Political Parties in Norway. Tavistock.

Ward, R. E. 1960. Urban-rural differences and the process of political modernization in Japan: A case study. Economic Development and Political Change, 9:135-65.

Ward, R. E. 1978. Japan's political system, 2nd ed. Englewood Cliffs, New Jersey: Prentice Hall.

Watanuki, J. 1967. Patterns of politics in present-day Japan. In S. M. Lipset and S. Rokkan (eds.), Party systems and voter alignments, New York: The Free Press.

White, J. W. 1973. Political implications of cityward migration: Japan as an exploratory test case. In H. Eckstein, T. Gurr, and Z. Zolberb (eds.), Sage professional papers in comparative politics. Beverly Hills: Sage, 5-59.

POLITICAL PARTICIPATION AND
POLICY PREFERENCE IN JAPAN

Soo Young Auh

Since World War II Japan has experienced an explosion in citizen political participation. In 1960, in the greatest mass movement in its political history, millions of Japanese participated directly in the Anti-Security Treaty Movement.[1] They signed petitions, engaged in work stoppages, and demonstrated in the Tokyo streets. More recently, environmental pollution concerns have led thousands to participate in a "citizen's movement" in which a variety of demonstrations, strikes, and petition drives have occurred.[2]

Political participation communicates citizen needs and desires to the government and helps express citizen preferences regarding the formulation of public policies. It is one of the main channels through which government decision-makers become aware of citizen preferences and are thus motivated to respond (Verba and Nie 1972:267-68; Verba, Nie, and Kim 1978:286-309). In this study, political participation refers to all those activities through which citizens either pay attention to others' political opinions or express their own political views in an attempt to influence governmental decision-making.[3] Our basic assumption is that government leaders will respond to citizen

---

I wish to express my gratitude to Professors M. Kent Jennings, Ronald F. Inglehart, and Richard K. Beardsley for their comments and suggestions, and to Professors Robert E. Ward and Akira Kubota for making the data upon which this study is based available, through the Inter-University Consortium for Political and Social Research.
1. The most comprehensive account and analysis in English of the 1960 political event appears in Packard 1966. See also Scalapino and Masumi 1962 (Ch. 5), and Krauss 1974.
2. See Simcock 1972; see also various articles in Nihon Seiji Gakkai 1974; Chihō Jichi Kyōkai 1974; and Matsubara 1976.
3. For similar definitions, see Verba, Nie, and Kim 1971:9-11; Verba and Nie 1972:2-3; Matthews and Prothro 1966:37-38; Milbrath 1965:5-38; and Milbrath and Goel 1977:2 and 5-34.

preferences communicated through political participation in a democratic system. But it is not assumed that increased participation necessarily results in greater influence in contemporary Japan, where politics tends to be broadly polarized around two ideological groups and the ruling conservative party has been in power for more than two decades.

The aim of this study is not to consider whether and to what degree political participation makes governmental leaders responsive to citizen demands. Rather, its purpose is to investigate the degree to which participation is related to citizen preferences. We can, however, explore two other questions:

1) Do those who participate in various political activities hold different policy positions from the population as a whole?

2) Do those attached to the various parties hold different policy positions from each other?

The study is based upon data drawn from the survey conducted by Robert E. Ward and Akira Kubota dealing with the 1967 Japanese general election. The original sample consisted of 1,973 respondents, including 177 youths 15 through 19 years of age. However, this study will analyze only the adult portion of the sample, the 1,796 citizens of voting age, 20 years old and above.

Patterns of Participation

As in other nations, the proportion of Japanese citizens active in politics varies widely depending on the type of participation examined. Electoral participation is relatively high: on average, 73 percent of the eligible voters turned out in the 15 general (Lower House) elections from 1946 to 1980, and the turnout in local elections is generally even higher (Bureau of Statistics 1979:452-53; Asahi Shimbun Sha 1980:266-68). However, the rate falls off quickly when we examine more active forms of participation, as may be seen in Table 1.[4]

---

4. The percentages reported in Table 1 are based on an unweighted N of 1,823 cases but are almost identical with those based on weighted cases.

TABLE 1
Percentage of Respondents Who Reported
Twelve Political Participation Activities

Types of Political Participation	Percent
Voted in 1967 Lower House election	81.0
Voted in 1963 Lower House election[a]	66.9
Watched political news on television[a]	44.0
Discussed politics with others	39.4
Read political coverage in newspapers[a]	35.7
Read political news in magazines[a]	19.5
Had ever marched in the streets	12.0
Attended campaign meetings in 1967 election	11.7
Participated in rallies or petition drives during Anti-Security Treaty Movement, 1960	7.6
Had ever tried to persuade someone of the best way to vote	6.3
Had ever given money to help a political cause or election campaign	6.1
Worked for party or candidate in 1967 election	3.0
N = 1823	

Note:
a. Variable originally containing more than two categories has been dichotomized.

It is clear from the frequency distributions that most political participation activities were performed by only a small segment of the Japanese citizenry. In fact, voting in elections to the House of Representatives was the only political activity in which a majority of Japanese citizens engaged. Slightly more than one-third of the respondents reported that they followed political affairs in newspapers or discussed politics with others. Fewer than 20 percent of the citizens participated in 7 of the 12 categories.

This pattern is explained by findings from research on popular attitudes. As Richardson (1974:93-94) has shown, most Japanese citizens have passive attitudes toward active political participation. When Japanese voters were asked to state the best method of expressing opinions and articulating demands at any level of politics, most resondents said they would simply "rely on their vote"; only a few countenanced more active forms of political participation. In response to a question on the "best thing to do to get one's political desires realized," 39 percent of the respondents in a mixed urban and rural district near Tokyo answered that they would "elect a good Diet member." An additional 18 percent said they could best profit by "depending on the efforts of political parties." Only 4 percent felt it would be best to "form a group and try to realize our desires through its activities."

Even given the low percentage of citizens active in politics, if participants emerged proportionately from all subgroups of the population—socioeconomic classes, age groups, urban and rural areas, and so forth—decision-makers will be presented with an unbiased sample of the citizenry (Verba and Nie 1972:267-69). Moreover, regardless of the distribution of participation among subgroups, if the policy preferences of active participants closely resemble those of the population as a whole, decision-makers will receive an accurate representation of public opinion. In Japan, as we will see, neither of these conditions hold: both the social characteristics and the policy preferences of active political participants are quite distinctive. (For details, see Auh 1978.)

For this study, the participant population will be defined broadly enough to encompass both active and passive participants, from those who engage in a single political act to those who constantly perform many political activities.[5] In order to identify the participant population we will employ the twelve political activities cited in Table 1. Combining these, we can identify four distinct participation types: 1) the least active type, those who engage in one activity or none at all; 2) the intermediate type, those who undertake two or three activities; 3) the active type, those who involve themselves in four or five activities; and 4) the most active type, participants in six or more activities. These four types make up the following proportions of the population: 1) least active, 19 percent; 2) intermediate, 39 percent; 3) active, 28 percent; and 4) most active, 15 percent.

Demographic Characteristics of the Four Participation Types

Table 2 portrays the demographic characteristics of the four participant types. Large numbers of the youngest and oldest voters are found in the least active group. About one-third of the least active participants are in the 20-30 age group, and one-quarter are over 60 years of age. In addition, the educational level of the least active type is very low. Slightly less than half received only an elementary education, while less than one-tenth are college-

---

5. The construction of our participant groups is based on the Verba and Nie method; see Verba and Nie 1972:269-70.

TABLE 2
Comparison of the Four Participant Types:
Demographic Characteristics (Percentages)

	Least Active	Intermediate	Active	Most Active	Total	N
AGE						
20-30	32	21	21	19	23	412
31-40	16	29	27	35	27	485
41-50	14	20	24	24	21	375
51-60	14	15	18	12	15	280
61+	25	15	11	11	15	271
Total	100	101	101	101	101	
N	344	712	501	266		1,823
EDUCATION						
Elementary	41	40	33	24	35	589
Jr. High	27	18	20	13	19	317
Sr. High	25	31	31	30	30	493
College	8	11	17	34	16	265
Total	101	100	101	101	100	
N	269	657	481	257		1,664
SOCIOECONOMIC STATUS						
Lower SES	48	40	27	19	34	550
Middle SES	42	45	52	58	49	784
Upper SES	10	15	22	23	17	281
Total	100	100	101	100	100	
N	257	638	470	250		1,615
SEX						
Male	31	36	59	79	48	866
Female	70	64	41	21	52	950
Total	101	100	100	100	100	
N	341	709	500	266		1,816
COMMUNITY TYPE						
Rural Areas	39	36	29	31	34	610
Small Cities	35	40	41	38	39	698
Big Cities	26	24	30	31	27	480
Total	100	100	100	100	100	
N	339	698	493	258		1,788

educated. The least active type is composed predominately of women and lower socioeconomic status individuals; it is also slightly more rural than the other three types.[6]

The most active type comprises a higher percentage of middle-aged citizens: over 50 percent of the most active participants are 31-50 years of age. Educational levels in this type are the highest of the four, with college-educated individuals comprising one-third and high-school-educated slightly less than one-third of the group. This type is composed mainly of middle-status males and is almost evenly distributed in rural areas, small cities, and large cities.

The remaining two types, intermediate and active, have similar demographic backgrounds, whose characteristics fall between those of the least active and most active types. The actives have slightly higher educational backgrounds, include more higher status persons, urbanites, and men than the intermediate type. Age distribution within these two types is very similar.

The demographic characteristics of the four types clearly show that politically more active Japanese are distinctive in education, status, age, and sex, rather than coming proportionately from every sector of society. The more active types are composed largely of well-educated, middle-status, middle-aged males. If participation transmits citizen preferences and demands to political leaders, the voices of the poorly-educated, lower-status, and elderly are not likely to be easily heard.

Participation and Policy Preference

We may now ask whether there are differences in policy preferences among the four participant types. The problem of selecting the correct policy issues for analysis is a difficult and complex one,[7] but happily Ward and Kubota included five quite appropriate issues in their survey:

---

6. The measure of socioeconomic status is a simple additive index. It was based on the educational level of respondents and the occupational status and income of the head of the respondent's household. Each of the variables was standardized and then summed, giving equal weight to education, income, and occupation.

7. For the debate on "issues and nonissues," see Bachrach and Baratz 1963, Wolfinger 1971, and Frey 1971.

1) Social Welfare spending: If the government has a choice between reducing taxes and spending more on social welfare, which should it do?

2) Constitutional amendment: Should the Japanese constitution be revised, or should it remain as it is?

3) Self-Defense Forces: Should Japan maintain the Self-Defense Forces as they are now, expand them, or dissolve them?

4) Conscription system: Should Japan set up a conscription system sometime in the near future or not?

5) The U.S. - Japan Security Treaty: Should the U.S. - Japan Security Treaty be strengthened, weakened, or abolished?

Each of these needs a few words of explanation.

The social welfare issue is one of the most important economic problems in the high-growth Japanese economy. Since the end of World War II, Japan has experienced a high level of growth, a high level of investment in plants and equipment, and a high level of exports. Since rapid economic growth has resulted in increased employment, higher income, and an international balance of payments surplus, Japan faces a growing demand to allocate more resources to the improvement of social welfare. There is pressure to provide better public housing, greater social security benefits, and more extensive medical insurance. However, in 1967 at least, most Japanese agreed in principle that more welfare spending was desirable, so the issue was not particularly contentious.

The other four issues have all sparked more debate. The constitution has been controversial throughout the postwar era both because of its origins (many perceive it as having been forced on Japan by the American Occupation authorities) and because of its many relatively liberal provisions covering such areas as civil rights, local autonomy, the position of the emperor, and especially the renunciation of war and the use of military force in Article 9.[8] Revision of the constitution was accordingly a high-priority goal among many leaders of the Liberal Democratic Party (LDP) and other conservatives throughout the 1950s and 1960s, and was strongly opposed by the progressives. (See Sissons 1961, Ward 1965, and Fukui 1968.) However, the intensity

---

8. For an excellent study of the present Japanese constitution, see Ward 1956; see also Ward 1967:83-85; McNelly 1959; Satō 1957; Kawai 1960:51-70; and Fukui 1970:198-226.

of feeling about the issue may have declined somewhat by the time of the 1967 survey examined here.

The next two issues, the Self-Defense Forces and conscription, have been controversial both in themselves and as a constitutional dispute, since their relationship to Article 9 is problematic. Public opinion has been sharply divided on whether, or to what extent, Japan should maintain military power, although over time acceptance of the Self-Defense Forces has increased (Emmerson and Humphreys 1973:9). The Mutual Security Treaty with the United States raises similar constitutional problems and has certainly been the most controversial issue in postwar Japanese politics. Its revision in 1960 touched off the widespread demonstrations that prevented President Eisenhower's visit to Japan and drove Prime Minister Kishi from power. The treaty remained a lively issue in 1967, since progressives were then gearing up for 1970, when under the 1960 provisions the treaty could be abrogated.

Let us compare the various activist types regarding their policy preferences on the five issues discussed above. The data are displayed in Figures 1 and 2. Figure 1-A presents the proportions of respondents who opted for increased welfare in response to the question about whether the government should spend more money on welfare or reduce taxes. Here, a higher proportion of activists favors spending more money on welfare. Less than half of the less active participants favor welfare spending, while slightly less than 60 percent of the two more active types approve. However, we may conclude that there is not a very significant difference in welfare preference between activist participants and the population as a whole.

In Figure 1-B we present the proportion of those who said the existing constitution should be revised. Of the least active and most active types, the same proportion of respondents favor revision (27%). A slightly greater proportion of the more active type favors revision, but here too there is little significant difference.

Policy preferences on the defense and foreign policy issues are presented in Figure 2. In the case of the Self-Defense Forces issues, for the sake of simplicity, we have presented only two of several preferences: 1) the proportion of those who want to expand the Self-Defense Forces; and 2) the proportion of those in favor of abolishing them. Of the four participant types, the most active one favors expansion the least. Interestingly, the least active type is also opposed to expansion. Both of these groups are more opposed to expanding the Self-Defense Forces than are either the intermediate or active types.

FIGURE 1

POLICY PREFERENCES ON WELFARE POLICY AND REVISION
OF CONSTITUTION

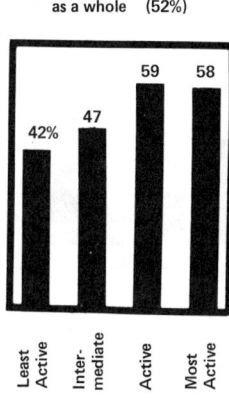
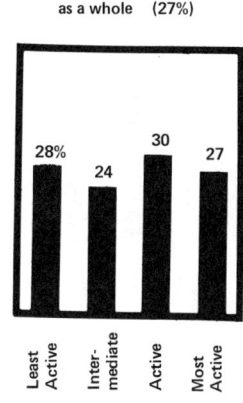

(A) Welfare

Proportion saying that the
government should spend
more on welfare.

(B) Revision of Constitution

Proportion saying that the
constitution should be
revised.

These tendencies become more visible on the question of abolishing the Self-Defense Forces. Slightly less than one-quarter of the most active type favor dissolution, while only 6 percent of the intermediate and 9 percent of the active types favor it. Concerning the related issue of conscription revival, once more the most active type is least in favor; the remaining three types show very similar preferences.

It is on the issue of the security treaty between the United States and Japan that participation really produces a difference in preference. The more active participants tend to be less favorably disposed toward strengthening the treaty and more inclined toward abolishing it. The proportion of those who favor strengthening the treaty decreases with an increase in political activity. Only 15 percent of the most active type favors increasing the treaty's strength, while 28 percent of the least active and 26 percent of the intermediate types are so disposed. Similarly, the proportion of those who

Figure 2

Policy Preferences on Self Defense Forces, Conscription System, and U.S.–Japan Mutual Security Treaty

Population as a whole (17%)

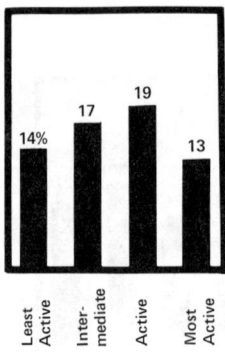

(A) Self Defense Forces

Proportion saying that the Self Defense Forces should be expanded

Population as a whole (10%)

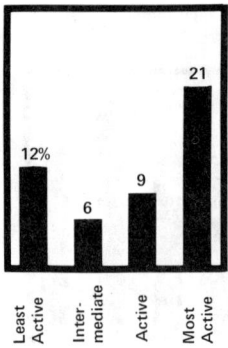

(B) Self Defense Forces

Proportion saying that the Self Defense Forces should be abolished.

Population as a whole (11%)

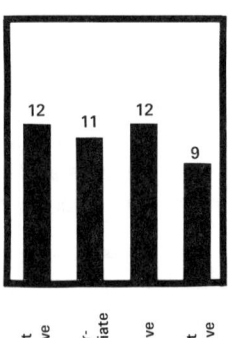

(C) Conscription System

Proportion saying that a conscription system should be set up.

Population as a whole (22%)

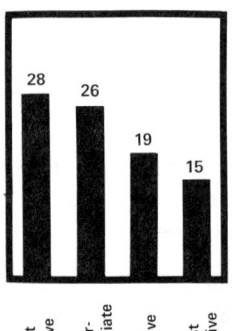

(D) U.S.–Japan Security Treaty

Proportion saying that the U.S.–Japan Security Treaty should be strengthened.

Population as a whole (15%)

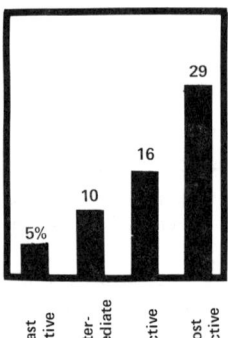

(E) U.S.–Japan Security Treaty

Proportion saying that the U.S.–Japan Security Treaty should be abolished.

favor abolishing the security treaty increases with political activity. As much as one-third of the most active type say they favor abolition, while only one-twentieth of the least active type desires it. Only 15 percent of the population as a whole are in favor of abrogating the treaty. Therefore, it appears that, as far as the Self-Defense Forces and the security treaty are concerned, political participation does make a significant difference in preference.

Defense issues stand in sharp contrast to the welfare issue, where participation does not make much difference in preference. This contrast may stem from many factors. First, all five major political parties have very similar platforms on welfare, while party policies on the Self-Defense Forces and the U.S. - Japan Security Treaty diverge greatly. As the demographic characteristics of the four participant types show, the most active type is made up of the better-educated and the city-dwellers (compared to the least active type). Highly-educated urban citizens in Japan tend to be identified with progressive parties, while the least active citizens tend to be poorly-educated, elderly, female, and rural, and more often identify with the ruling conservative party. These factors may be responsible for the significant difference in preference on defense and foreign policy issues between inactive and active citizens. This phenomenon will be more clearly visible in the next section of this study, when we deal with the impact of political party preferences and participation on issue positions.

There is an interesting contrast between Japan and the United States in attitudes toward welfare. When Verba and Nie classified American respondents into six different levels of participation, they found that, for the welfare issue, the "activist population is more in favor of individualistic solutions and somewhat less in favor of government intervention in welfare matters than is the population as a whole" (Verba and Nie 1972:277). Conversely, Japanese activists appear to prefer greater government intervention in welfare. In our classification of Japanese respondents, 59 percent of the active and 58 percent of the most active types favor spending more money on welfare, compared with just 42 percent of the least active and 47 percent of the intermediate types. Slightly more than half of the entire population favors governmental involvement in welfare. Apparently more Japanese activists are sympathetic to socialist views of the welfare issue. A possible reason may be that well-educated Japanese tend to be exposed, to a large extent, to socialism and marxism during their college careers.[9]

9. For excellent accounts of the history of Marxism among Japanese intellectuals, see Ike 1964, and Krauss 1974.

The Role of Political Parties

So far, we have not considered the impact of political parties on their supporters' policy preferences. We have simply compared preferences according to level of activity. One's political orientation, conservative or progressive, may play a crucial role in the formation of opinions regarding specific issues, defense and foreign policy in particular, especially since Japanese politics is sharply polarized along the left-to-right dimension. The Japan Socialist Party (JSP), for example, educates its supporters in socialist ideology, helps to develop their progressive political orientation, and guides their political preferences on specific issues. The LDP orients its supporters in the other direction.

In this sense, if any difference exists in policy preferences between the active and less active population, it may well be the result of the relationship between the left-right ideological orientation and participation. In other words, it may not be the participation that causes the difference in preference, but that both participation and policy preferences are the result of a third factor, ideological orientation (or the impact of party identification). However, we are not so much concerned with the causal relationship between participation and policy preference as with our central question: if citizens with different ideological orientations participate at different rates, are the policy preferences which are thereby carried into the decision-making process correspondingly affected?

Our examination of the effects of political parties on policy preferences must focus on the LDP and the JSP, the two largest parties, because we lack a sufficient number of respondents for the smaller parties. Their policy positions differ considerably. As noted earlier, the conservative leaders of the LDP had attempted to revise the constitution in whole or part, while the JSP had made every effort to stop its revision. The LDP advocated strengthening the Self-Defense Forces and a close military alliance with the United States for national security. The JSP, on the other hand, favored unarmed neutralism and abolition of the Self-Defense Forces and the U.S. - Japan Security Treaty. There was less avowed difference on the welfare issue, although the JSP advocated more extensive welfare policies, such as free medical insurance, a higher minimum wage, expansions of social security and so forth (Jiyū Minshutō 1968:19-25; Nihon Shakaitō Seisaku Shingikai 1966:18-45, 138-53).

95

Figure 3

Political Participation and Policy Preferences:
Impact of Political Party

(A) Welfare

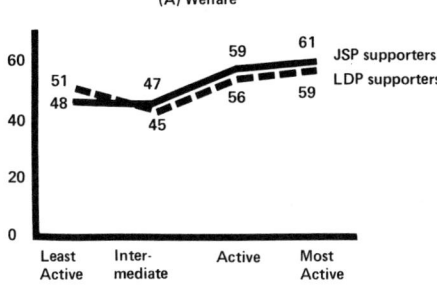

Proportion saying that the government
should spend more on welfare.

Population as a whole (52%)

(C) Self-Defense Forces

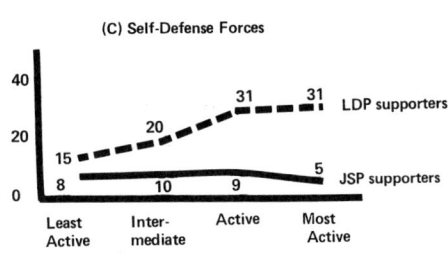

Proportion saying that the Self Defense
Forces should be expanded.

Population as a whole (17%)

(B) Revision of Constitution

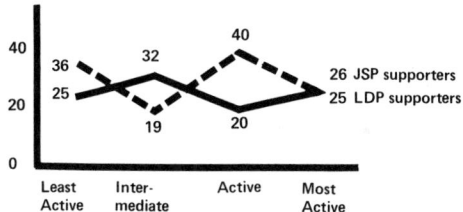

Proportion saying that the constitution
should be revised.

Population as a whole (27%)

(D) Self Defense Forces

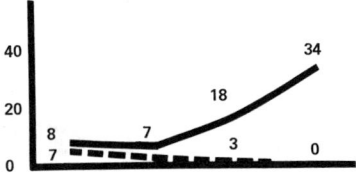

Proportion saying that the Self Defense
Forces should be abolished.

Population as a whole (10%)

Figure 3 (cont)

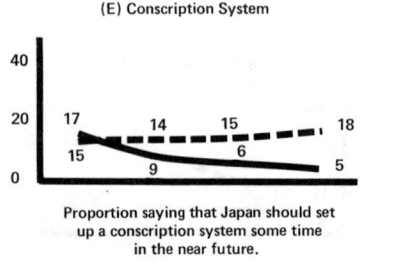

(E) Conscription System

Proportion saying that Japan should set up a conscription system some time in the near future.

Population as a whole (11%)

(F) U.S.–Japan Security Treaty

Proportion saying that the U.S.–Japan Mutual Security Treaty should be strengthened.

Population as a whole (22%)

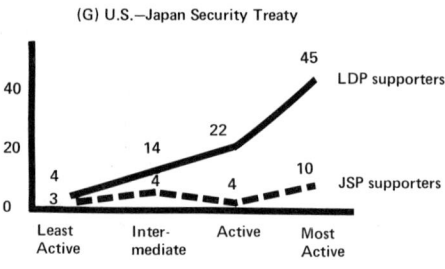

(G) U.S.–Japan Security Treaty

Proportion saying that that the U.S.–Japan Mutual Security Treaty should be abolished.

Population as a whole (16%)

The relevant data are presented in Figure 3, which presents the preferences of LDP and JSP identifiers at different levels of political activity. Figure 3-A shows that JSP identifiers are only slightly more in favor of increased spending on welfare than LDP identifiers, and that differences in participation do not have much impact. Regarding constitutional revision, the impact of political parties on preferences is irregular. The least active and active types among LDP supporters are more in favor of revision, but the intermediate and most active types among JSP supporters also favor revision. Therefore, we do not find a clear pattern with regard to this issue.

In contrast to these two issues, the impact of political parties on the preferences of their supporters in the areas of defense and foreign policy is clearly visible. Interestingly, the effect of political parties becomes greater as their supporters become active. Figure 3-C shows that the LDP supporters are much more in favor of expanding the Self-Defense Forces than the JSP supporters. This difference in preference between the identifiers with the two parties increases with rising political activity, because the proportion of those saying the Self-Defense Forces should be expanded increases with the rise in political activity among LDP supporters and decreases among JSP supporters. The attitude favoring abolition of the Self-Defense Forces shown in Figure 3-D manifests the same pattern. The only difference is direction: among LDP supporters, the proportion of those saying the Self-Defense Forces should be abolished decreases with rise in political activity, while among JSP supporters, the proportion increases as their political activity rises. Regarding the issue of reviving the conscription system, LDP supporters are more in favor of this proposal than JSP supporters, but here participation apparently makes a significant difference only for JSP identifiers. Still, the differences between party identifiers are clearly widest among the most active.

The issue of strengthening the U.S. - Japan Security Treaty, however, is less clearcut. LDP identifiers are more in favor, but the relationship of activity to preference is curvilinear. The least active are most in favor of strengthening the treaty, the two intermediate types less so, and the most active type falls between. Among JSP supporters, the favorable attitude toward treaty strengthening generally decreases proportionately with increased political participation. Conversely, the proportion of those in favor of abrogating the treaty (Figure 3-G) among JSP supporters increases sharply as political activity heightens. The difference in preference between LDP and JSP supporters in the least-active category is the smallest, the difference becoming greater with increased political participation. However, as with treaty strengthening, the proportion of LDP supporters favoring abrogation is relatively flat with regard to participation. This somewhat anomalous result occurs because many LDP supporters, including active participants, actually favor the status quo over either strengthening or abrogating the treaty.

The findings in this section may be summarized as follows: first, supporters of the two parties have nearly identical opinions on welfare expansion (a nonideological issue among the Japanese in 1967) and display a curiously mixed pattern with regard to constitutional revision, but diverge sharply on security issues. Of course, it is this policy area that has seen the most dramatic conflicts between the two parties throughout the postwar era. Second, and most interesting, it is those people most politically active who generally adhere most to their parties' platforms. In fact, the gap between relatively inactive LDP and JSP supporters is often quite insignificant.

Implications

The wide differences in preference on defense and foreign policy issues between activists of the two major parties have been a source of political unrest in Japan. These differences stem from competing political ideologies and Weltanschauungen and are not easily narrowed. Activists are highly visible to the public and their divergent views are well-publicized by the mass media. Whenever these defense and foreign policy issues become salient, the activists of both parties will clash. However, we should note that in recent years public acceptance of the Self-Defense Forces has grown, and the Security Treaty too is no longer quite such a burning issue (Emmerson and Humphreys 1973:75-106).

Political participation is a major means for citizens to transmit their policy preferences to decision-makers. In this way, political leaders become aware of the needs and desires of citizens, and may respond to them. It is for this reason that participation is highly valued in a democratic society. But all citizens are not participants. Moreover, the preferences of participants differ according to their level of political activity. On controversial issues, the supporters of the ruling party differ widely in their preferences from those of the opposition parties in proportion to the level of political activity. The participators are not a random sample of the population; therefore, their preferences are skewed in a certain direction. Consequently, participation does not reflect the preferences of the entire population. Political leaders are more likely to listen to opinions of the activists around them and to the preferences of supporters who contact them.

References

Asahi Shinbun Sha. 1980. Asahi Shinbun Nenkan.

Auh, Soo Young. 1978. Japanese political participation in comparative perspective. Unpublished Ph.D. dissertation, Department of Political Science, University of Michigan.

Bachrach, Peter, and Morton S. Baratz. 1963. Decisions and nondecisions: An analytical framework. American Political Science Review, 57:632-42.

Bureau of Statistics (Japan). 1979. Statistical Yearbook. Office of the Prime Minister.

Chihō Jichi Kyōkai. 1974. Jūmin undō chōsa hōkokusho (Reports on the citizens' movement), Vols. 1 and 2. Tokyo.

Emmerson, John K., and Leonard A. Humphreys. 1973. Will Japan rearm? Stanford: AEI-Hoover Policy Studies.

Frey, Frederick W. 1971. Comment (on Wolfinger 1971). American Political Science Review, 65:1081-1101.

Fukui, Haruhiro. 1968. The Liberal Democratic Party and constitutional revision. In D.C.S. Sissons, ed., Papers on modern Japan. Canberra: Department of International Relations, Australian National University.

_____. 1970. Party in Power. Berkeley: University of California Press.

Matsubara Haruo. 1976. Jūmin undō no ronri (Theories of the citizens' movement). Tokyo.

Ike, Nobutaka. 1964. The political role of Japanese intellectuals. Journal of Social and Political Ideas in Japan, 2.

Jiyū Minshūtō. 1968. Jiyū minshūtō nenpō, 1966-1967 (The annual report of the Liberal Democratic Party, 1966-1967). Tokyo.

Kawai, Kazuo. 1960. Japan's American interlude. Chicago: University of Chicago Press.

Krauss, Ellis S. 1974. Japanese radicals revisited. Berkeley: University of California Press.

Matthews, Donald R., and James W. Prothro. 1966. Negroes and the new southern politics. New York: Harcourt, Brace and World, Inc.

McNelly, Theodore. 1959. The Japanese constitution: Child of the cold war. Political Science Quarterly, 74:179-95.

Milbrath, Lester W. 1965. Political participation: How and why do people get involved in politics. Chicago: Rand McNally & Co.

Milbrath, Lester W., and M. Goel. 1977. Political participation. Chicago: Rand McNally & Co.

Nihon Seiji Gakkai. 1974. Nenpō Seijigaku (The annals of the Japan Political Science Association). Tokyo.

Nihon Shakaitō Seisaku Shingikai. 1966. Shakaitō no seisaku (Policies of the Japan Socialist Party). Tokyo.

Packard, George R. 1966. Protest in Tokyo. Princeton: Princeton University Press.

Richardson, Bradley M. 1974. The political culture of Japan. Berkeley: University of California Press.

Satō, Tatsuo. 1957. The origin and development of the draft constitution of Japan. Contemporary Japan, 24:1-55.

Scalapino, Robert A., and Junnosuke Masumi. 1965. Parties and politics in contemporary Japan. Berkeley: University of California Press.

Simcock, Bradford L. 1972. Environmental pollution and citizens' movements: The social sources and significance of anti-pollution protest in Japan. Area development in Japan, 5:13-22.

Sissons, D.C.S. 1961. The pacifist clause of the Japanese constitution: Legal and political problems of rearmament. International Affairs (London), 37:45-59.

Verba, Sidney, and Norman Nie. 1972. Participation in America. New York: Harper & Row.

Verba, Sidney, Norman Nie and Jae-on Kim. 1978. Participation and political equality. Cambridge: Cambridge University Press.

_____. 1971. The modes of democratic participation: a cross-national comparison. Comparative Political Series, 2:9-11.

Ward, Robert E. 1956. The origin of the present Japanese constitution. American Political Science Review, 50:980-1010.

_____. 1965. The Commission on the Constitution and prospects for constitutional change in Japan. Journal of Asian Studies, 24:401-29.

_____. 1967. Japan's political system. New Jersey: Prentice-Hall, Inc.

Wolfinger, Raymond E. 1971. "Non-decisions" and the study of local politics. American Political Science Review, 65:1063-80.

CANDIDATES AND PARTY IMAGES:
RECRUITMENT TO THE JAPANESE HOUSE OF REPRESENTATIVES,
1958 - 1972

Jung-Suk Youn

A political party is known by its candidates. Policy pronouncements and legislative actions help project the image of a party to the public, but at election time the party's character must be personified in its individual candidates. It is likely that legislative candidates are an unusually important factor in shaping party images in Japan, given the lack of national-level candidates to attract voters' attention, and the tendency of Japanese to look to individual characteristics rather than party identification or issue evaluations in making voting decisions.[1]

To begin to understand this relationship between candidate and party in Japan, we need systematic information on who runs for office. Previous research on Japanese elites and political recruitment has focused on prime ministers (Ryang 1973), cabinet members (Miyake 1964; Barhaugh 1976), and Dietmen (Sugimori 1968; Nishikawa 1974), but studies of candidates are rare (Kim 1967; Shiratori 1970; Blaker 1976). As part of a larger study of political recruitment and nominating behavior (Youn 1977), I collected biographical data on the 1,649 party candidates who contested the six general (Lower House) elections from 1958 to 1972.[2] The purpose of this article is simply to

---

1. This tendency may be due to psychological factors or to the Japanese electoral system. See Richardson (1974) and the article by Rochon in this volume.
2. This figure includes 18 candidates who were double counted because they ran in two districts. Another 600 or so ran only as independent or "minor party" candidates during this period and are not included in my analysis. Biographical information was drawn from general Who's Who publications, information on Dietmen compiled by the House of Representatives and private organizations, party materials, and other sources; for a complete list see Youn (1977:265-67).

describe the candidates of the five major parties in terms of their electoral experience, age, education, occupation, and organizational affiliations.

Table 1 gives the distribution of these candidates by party and by whether they first ran before or after 1958; it also includes the percentages of candidates who were elected at least once among those who first ran after 1958.[3] This table reflects important differences in party nomination practices. The Liberal Democratic Party (LDP) and to a lesser extent the Japan Socialist Party (JSP) run more than one candidate in nearly all districts, and so must carefully limit their nominations to avoid spreading the available vote too thin. This practice results in a relatively high success ratio. The Democratic Socialist Party (DSP) and the Clean Government Party (CGP) run one candidate in each district that offers a good prospect for success; clearly the CGP has made better guesses. The Japan Communist Party (JCP) views elections not only as a route to Diet power but also as an important tool for political education, and accordingly runs a candidate in every election district even when there is no real chance of success. Accordingly, its success ratio is quite low.

TABLE 1
Party Distribution of Candidates
and Success Ratios

Parties	Total Number of Candidates	Pre-1958 Number of Candidates	Post-1958 Number of Candidates	Percent Elected
LDP	692	387	305	77.0
JSP	380	163	217	70.0
DSP	179	41	138	23.2
CGP	87	0	87	56.3
JCP	311	61	250	15.5
Total	1,649	652	997	50.8

These differences in nomination strategies and electoral success result in considerable variation among the parties in the electoral experience of their candidates. Table 2 shows the distribution of all official party candidates in the 1972 election by year of first campaign. Nearly half the 1972 LDP candidates began their electoral careers in 1958 or earlier, while

---

3. This "success ratio" cannot be calculated from my data for the pre-1958 period because unsuccessful candidates who did not run in 1958 or thereafter are excluded.

nearly half the Communists ran for the first time in 1972. Of course, much of the variation is explained by the universal custom of almost always renominating incumbents; the LDP always has the most incumbents running in each election, and the JCP has the lowest proportion of incumbents among its candidates.

TABLE 2
First Election Contested by 1972 Candidates, by Party

Year	LDP	JSP	DSP	CGP	JCP
Pre-1958	42.8%	26.7%	22.2%		5.0%
1958	5.7	9.3	3.2		2.5
1960	8.2	9.9	6.3		4.1
1963	9.3	7.5	4.8		8.3
1967	10.2	14.9	19.0	44.8%	14.0
1969	12.2	11.8	17.5	43.1	22.3
1972	11.6	19.9	27.0	12.1	43.8
Total	100.0%	100.0%	100.0%	100.0%	100.0
N	352	181	63	58	121

TABLE 3
Age Distribution of Candidates by Party
in Six Elections

Age Bracket	Total	LDP	JSP	DSP	JCP
The 1958 Election					
20-29	0.3%	0.5%			
30-39	6.1	2.7	6.1%		
40-49	26.2	19.5	35.6		19.5%
50-59	42.2	41.3	40.9		30.9
60-69	19.8	27.4	15.4		48.7
70+	5.4	8.6	2.0		0.9
Total	100.0%	100.0%	100.0%		100.0%
N	791	431	247		113
The 1960 Election					
20-29	0.1%	0.2%			
30-39	8.8	4.7	5.8%	11.5%	22.6%
40-49	21.3	17.2	30.9	20.9	27.8
50-59	44.0	41.2	42.4	48.9	46.1
60-69	20.6	28.4	16.2	17.6	2.6
70+	5.2	8.3	2.6	2.1	0.9
Total	100.0%	100.0%	99.9%	100.0%	100.0%
N	811	408	191	96	115

TABLE 3 (continued)

Age Bracket	Total	LDP	JSP	DSP	CGP	JCP
			The 1963 Election			
20-29	0.4%	1.0%				
30-39	8.3	4.6	4.6%	10.5%		26.1%
40-49	20.3	15.5	26.9	24.6		20.9
50-59	39.0	35.5	44.6	33.3		46.1
60-69	25.3	33.7	19.8	26.3		6.1
70+	6.6	9.8	4.1	5.3		0.9
Total	99.9%	100.1%	100.0%	100.0%		100.1%
N	755	386	197	57		115
			The 1967 Election			
20-29	0.3%	0.5%				
30-39	6.3	4.9	1.4%	5.1%	28.1%	14.2%
40-49	25.1	17.7	27.6	18.6	50.0	40.0
50-59	32.3	28.5	42.4	40.7	18.8	25.8
60-69	27.6	34.2	24.8	27.1	3.1	20.0
70+	8.4	14.1	3.8	8.5		
Total	100.0%	99.9%	100.0%	100.0%	100.0%	100.0%
N	789	368	210	59	32	120
			The 1969 Election			
20-29	0.7%	0.8%	1.1%	2.4%		
30-39	10.3	6.4	1.1	7.1	49.6%	14.3%
40-49	28.4	17.6	32.4	27.1	39.2	48.7
50-59	30.4	31.4	41.1	40.0	4.1	19.4
60-69	23.5	30.8	23.2	18.6		16.8
70+	6.6	12.9	1.1	5.7		0.8
Total	99.9%	99.9%	100.0%	99.9%	99.9%	100.0%
N	805	357	185	70	74	119
			The 1972 Election			
20-29	0.1%	0.3%				
30-39	7.7	6.8	2.5%	12.7%	32.8%	14.9%
40-49	26.3	18.4	26.7	25.4	46.6	57.0
50-59	31.2	26.6	42.9	33.3	15.5	18.2
60-69	23.7	32.9	24.2	20.6	5.2	6.6
70+	9.0	15.0	3.7	7.9		3.3
Total	100.0%	100.0%	100.0%	99.9%	100.1%	100.0%
N	756	353	161	63	58	121

The practice of renominating incumbents also produces rather substantial differences among parties in the age of their candidates. Table 3 indicates that LDP candidates tend to be older than those of other parties, and that its proportion of candidates aged 60 or above increased somewhat between 1958 and 1972 (although the proportion of those under 50 remained about the same). Candidates of the CGP, and to a lesser extent those of the JCP (since 1960), are considerably younger. The entry of the CGP helped to lower the overall age profile of Japanese candidates: only about 30 percent of all party candidates were under age 50 prior to the 1969 election, but in that year the figure rose to 39.4 percent before dropping somewhat to 36.1 percent in 1972.

The propensity of parties to nominate women differs slightly, but, as Table 4 reveals, none can be considered particularly enlightened with regard to sexual balance. In general, Japanese Diet candidates were overwhelmingly middle-aged or elderly males.

TABLE 4
Sex

Sex	Total	LDP	JSP	DSP	CGP	JCP
Male	97.7%	98.4%	96.8%	96.1%	96.6%	98.4%
Female	2.3	1.6	3.2	3.9	3.4	1.6
Total	100.0%	100.0%	100.0%	100.0%	100.0%	100.0%
N	1,649	692	380	179	87	311

As is true in other political systems, Japanese candidates tend to be better educated than the general population. But, as Table 5 indicates, the parties differ rather sharply in this respect. The LDP had a high proportion of university graduates and only a few of its candidates had not progressed beyond elementary school. The JCP shows the reverse pattern, but even so, nearly half the Communist candidates had some college experience. Further differences emerge when one examines the types of universities attended by candidates (Table 6). Here, the LDP and the JCP are most similar: of those who graduated from a university, more than half in both parties attended Tokyo University or one of the other prewar Imperial Universities, still the highest in status today. The CGP is notable in that about three-quarters of its university graduates attended private universities.

Similar differences appear when we examine occupational background. Here we must look into each candidate's biography to ascertain his principle occupation before becoming a professional politician. An occupation in this sense could be determined for 1,540 (93 percent) of the 1,649 party candidates, and these are shown in Table 7. The LDP drew over two-thirds of its candidates from either business or government, predominantly from the

TABLE 5
Educational Level

Level of Education	All Candidates	LDP	JSP	DSP	CGP	JCP
Elementary	10.3%	5.3%	12.9%	11.7%	3.4%	19.9%
Secondary	18.0	10.8	22.1	15.1	24.1	28.3
Jr. college or some univ.	14.9	11.8	17.6	10.6	20.7	19.3
Col. or univ. graduate	50.6	69.2	41.6	44.7	44.8	25.1
Unknown	6.2	2.7	5.8	17.9	6.9	7.4
Total	100.0%	99.8%	100.0%	100.0%	99.9%	100.0%
N	1,649	692	380	179	87	311

TABLE 6
Specific Universities

University	All Candidates	LDP	JSP	DSP	CGP	JCP
Public U.	49.0%	53.8%	40.2%	36.6%	26.1%	63.5%
(Tokyo U.)	30.2	38.3	19.4	19.4	4.3	30.1
(Other former Imp. U.)	12.8	10.5	14.5	13.9	6.6	23.7
(Other)	6.0	5.0	6.3	3.3	15.2	9.7
Private U.	48.6	44.5	55.2	59.1	73.9	35.5
Foreign U.	2.4	1.8	4.6	4.3		1.1
Total	100.0%	99.9%	100.0%	100.0%	100.0%	100.1%
N	912	506	174	93	46	93

Note: N excludes candidates who did not attend a university, or for whom the university is unknown.

upper levels. CGP candidates were drawn disproportionately from professional backgrounds, while many Communist candidates were full-time party or union activists. As might be expected, higher than average proportions of JSP candidates were low-level employees in business, government, or educational institutions before turning to politics.

In addition, nearly all candidates have experience more directly related to politics. Significant numbers in each party were active in local electoral politics prior to their move up to the national level, usually in legislative rather than executive roles.[4] As Table 8 shows, the importance of this

---

4. The pattern among Upper House candidates differs; see Curtis (1976).

TABLE 7
Party Candidates by Positions Held Prior to Candidacy

Occupation and Positions Held	All Candidates	LDP	JSP	DSP	CGP	JCP
Business and Industry	33.6%	39.3%	28.4%	37.4%	35.6%	24.4%
Executive Level	26.2	37.9	18.7	27.4	27.6	8.4
Top Management (Major)*, President or Director (Middle)*	3.1	4.9	1.3	5.6	4.6	
Middle Management (Major), Top Management (Middle), President (Small)*	20.7	30.9	14.7	19.6	18.4	6.4
Lower Management	2.4	2.3	2.6	2.2	4.6	1.9
Staff Manager Level	4.5	1.4	6.6	3.9	6.9	8.7
Staff and Employees	2.9		3.2	6.1	1.1	7.4
Civil Service and Government Employees	17.5	29.0	11.1	11.7	9.2	5.5
Executive Level	9.5	19.5	3.4	4.5		0.3
Vice-Minister, Governor, Ambassador	3.8	8.1	1.3	1.7		
Division Chief, Mayor, Vice-Governor	5.9	11.4	2.1	2.8		0.3
Staff Manager Level	4.1	5.9	2.9	3.9	3.4	1.6
Section Chief (Central Government)	2.2	3.9	1.6	1.7		
Section Chief (Local Government)	1.9	2.0	1.3	2.2	3.4	1.6
Staff and Employees	2.1	0.7	4.7			2.9
Higher Civil Service in Colonies or Manchuria	1.8	2.9		3.4	2.3	0.6

107

TABLE 7 (continued)

Occupation and Positions Held	All Candidates	LDP	JSP	DSP	CGP	JCP
Education	<u>8.7</u>	<u>6.1</u>	<u>13.9</u>	<u>7.8</u>	<u>5.7</u>	<u>9.3</u>
Executive Level *Superintendent, President of University, Director of Private University, Head of Board of Education*	3.0	3.6	3.9	2.8	1.1	1.3
Principal, Professor, Member of Board of Education	0.8	1.7		1.1		
	2.2	1.9	3.9	1.7	1.1	1.3
Staff Manager Level *Head Teacher, Associate Professor, Special Lecturer*	1.0	0.7	1.8	1.7		1.0
Staff and Employees *Teacher, Assistant*	4.5	0.1	8.2	3.4	4.6	7.1
Police, Self-Defense Forces, and Prewar Military Career	<u>0.5</u>	<u>1.0</u>	<u>0.3</u>		<u>1.1</u>	
General, Admiral, Commander, Major	0.4	0.9				
Lieutenant, Ensign, Captain	0.1	0.1				
Corporal, Sergeant, NCO	0.1		0.3		1.1	
Transportation and Communications	<u>5.2</u>		<u>11.6</u>	<u>3.4</u>	<u>3.4</u>	<u>10.3</u>
Executive Level *Regional Head, Station Master, Post Office Manager*	0.1		0.3			
Staff Manager Level *Assistant Station Master, Deputy-Head of a Ward, Head of a Branch Office*	0.5		1.3	0.6		1.0

TABLE 7 (continued)

Occupation and Positions Held	All Candidates	LDP	JSP	DSP	CGP	JCP
Transportation and Communications (continued)						
Staff and Employees *Clerk, Technician, Permanently Employed Laborer*	4.5		10.0	2.8	3.4	9.3
Professionals *Lawyers, Physicians, Journalists, Writers*	13.6	13.4	14.2	12.8	20.7	11.6
Political Organizers and Union Activists *Full-time Party Staff, Union Office Staff*	14.3	9.2	12.9	15.6	5.7	28.9
Unknown	6.6	1.9	7.6	11.2	18.4	10.0
Total	100.0%	99.9%	100.0%	100.0%	100.0%	100.0%
N	1,649	692	380	179	87	311

* "Major" stands for the major industries and large corporations; "middle" stands for the middle-sized industries and a relatively large company; "small" stands for the small companies, incorporated or private proprietor.

channel to Diet candidacy varies among the parties: few JCP candidates but many CGP candidates previously served in prefectural or municipal assemblies. It should be noted that the likelihood of a given local politician running for the Diet is considerably lower for conservatives than for opposition party members, because an overwhelming majority of local assembly members are either LDP members or conservatively aligned independents.

TABLE 8
Local Electoral Experience

A. Prefectural Assembly

	All Candidates	LDP	JSP	DSP	CGP	JCP
Prior Exp.	21.8%	24.3%	31.3%	19.6%	31.0%	3.2%
No Exp.	76.9	75.0	68.2	76.0	69.0	94.9
Unknown	1.3	0.7	0.5	4.5	0.0	1.9
Total	100.0%	100.0%	100.0%	100.1%	100.0%	100.0%
N	1649	692	380	179	87	311

B. City-Town-Village Assembly

	All Candidates	LDP	JSP	DSP	CGP	JCP
Prior Exp.	19.0%	19.8%	20.3%	14.5%	40.2%	11.9%
No Exp.	79.7	79.5	79.2	81.0	59.8	86.2
Unknown	1.3	0.7	0.5	4.5	0.0	1.9
Total	100.0%	100.0%	100.0%	100.0%	100.0%	100.0%
N	1649	692	380	179	87	311

It is also interesting that, although over 90 percent of the candidates (for whom we have these data) of every party held some official post within their own party organizations, conservatives were much less likely to hold office in local organizations. Table 9 indicates that the proportion of LDP candidates who held party office only at the national level is twice that of the other parties, and the proportion of those holding only local office is less than half that of the other parties. These data well illustrate Curtis's (1971) observation that LDP candidates come in two types: nationally oriented (mainly ex-bureaucrats) and locally oriented (mainly local politicians). Journalists, businessmen, interest-group leaders, and others are found in either type, depending on whether their earlier careers were in Tokyo or the provinces. However, in Japan, even a nationally oriented politician cannot simply be assigned a "safe" conservative seat in any convenient election district. He must still be accepted by the prefectural party chapter, meaning that some local connections are usually necessary. A minimum qualification is local birth: Table 10 reveals the apparently paradoxical finding that, despite the large numbers of nationally oriented candidates in the LDP, conservatives were far more likely to have been born in or near their election districts than the candidates of other parties. This anomaly probably reflects the importance assigned to jimoto (locality) and perhaps to family factors among conservatives generally, especially in rural areas.[5] Of course, a much higher proportion of candidates in the LDP (and to a lesser extent in the JSP, which also shows a high proportion of local birth) run in rural districts.

TABLE 9
Posts in Party Organizations

Level	All Candidates	LDP	JSP	DSP	CGP	JCP
Local	30.9%	12.6%	31.8%	26.8%	32.2%	72.3%
Local & Nat'l HQ	20.7	15.2	29.7	27.4	42.5	12.2
Only Nat'l HQ	28.1	44.2	21.3	15.6	20.7	9.6
No Posts	4.2	7.4	2.4	2.8	2.3	0.6
Unknown	16.1	20.5	14.7	27.9	2.3	5.1
Total	100.0%	99.9%	99.9%	100.0%	100.0%	99.8%
N	1649	692	380	179	87	311

Candidates of the five political parties also differ markedly in their organizational affiliations. While the available biographical information is spotty for reporting ties to non-political organizations, significant participation was found for just over half the candidates. Table 11 list types of organization by party. LDP and DSP candidates are least likely to be affiliated; among LDP candidates with reported organizational ties, over half are attached to civic organizations (largely neighborhood associations) and over one-quarter to cooperatives (mainly agricultural). DSP candidates are fairly likely to be union members, though not to the extent of the two left-wing parties. In two parties, candidates are directly nominated by outside organizations.

---

5. For a brief account of how such factors are viewed by candidates, see the article by Yanagihashi in this volume.

TABLE 10
Birthplace of Party Candidates

	All Candidates	LDP	JSP	DSP	CGP	JCP
Local	68.1%	81.1%	68.2%	45.3%	42.5%	48.9%
Not local	18.2	13.3	21.1	20.7	24.1	22.5
Unknown	15.7	5.6	10.8	34.1	33.3	28.6
Total	100.0%	100.0%	100.1%	100.1%	99.9%	100.0%
N	1649	692	380	179	87	311

TABLE 11
Organizational Ties of Party Candidates

	All Candidates	LDP	JSP	DSP	CGP	JCP
Trade Unions	21.3%	0.9%	46.1%	26.3%		39.9%
Farmer Unions	9.5	2.9	18.7	8.4		18.1
Civic Organ.	12.8	20.2	8.9	7.8	2.3%	6.8
Cooperative Associations	5.5	9.2	4.7	2.2	1.1	1.3
Sōkagakkai	3.5				63.5	
Others	0.8	1.7	0.3	0.6		
None or Unknown	46.6	65.0	21.3	54.7	31.0	36.0
Total	100.0%	99.9%	100.0%	100.0%	99.9%	100.1%
N	1649	692	380	179	87	311

Until 1972, CGP candidates were directly chosen by the national Sōkagakkai leadership, and even afterward nearly all who have run for the Diet have been members of that lay Buddhist organization. Many JSP candidates are "sponsored" by local labor unions, and indeed the proportion of JSP candidates nominated in this way rose steadily, from 30.9 percent in 1958 to 55.3 percent in 1972.

Although the candidates of Japan's five major parties share some characteristics, we have discovered that they differ significantly in several respects. These differences are summarized in Table 12; the terms used are relative ones (that is, CGP candidates are young compared with those of other parties, not in an absolute sense). It is interesting that the tendencies revealed here generally correspond to images of the parties that one commonly encounters among Japanese voters. The LDP looks like an aging establishment, the JSP like a group of old-line union politicians, the CGP like a tool of the Sōkagakkai, and the Communists like a cadre party. The personality of the DSP appears blurry here, as indeed it often seems to Japanese voters.[7]

TABLE 12
Differences among Party Candidates: Summary

	LDP	JSP	DSP	CGP	JCP
Age	oldest	old	medium	youngest	young
Education	high	medium	medium	medium	low
Occupation	high level bureaucratic and business	low level private or public employee	no special characteristics	independent professional	party or union functionaries
National Electoral Experience	highest	high	medium	low	low
Local Political Experience	medium	high	medium	highest	low
Party Posts	national	mixed	mixed	mixed	local
Local Birth	high	medium	low	lowest	low
Organizational Ties	low: coops & civic orgs.	high: unions	low: unions	high: sokagakkai	medium: unions

None of these images is particularly favorable, and certainly each party would like to project a more positive personality. One effective way to do so would be to change their patterns of candidate nomination. However, one is struck by the extent to which variations in candidate characteristics among parties have been produced by factors that are extremely difficult to control. These external constraints include the exigencies of Japan's peculiar electoral system, the incumbents-first principle, dependence upon outside organizations for crucial resources, and the difficulty of finding attractive candidates when the chances of victory are low. In fact, the ability of the

---

7. These assertions are based on general observation, since I know of no systematic research on party images in this sense; however, see Nishihira (1972).

parties to choose candidates who would better contribute to image-building strategies is severely circumscribed. As noted by Strate in this volume, political parties find it difficult to broaden their bases of support, and often become "locked-in" to a particular, limited subculture within the electorate. We can speculate that such tendencies can only be reinforced by the patterns of nominating behavior outlined here.

References

Barhaugh, John H. 1976. Selection criteria for Japanese cabinet ministers. Unpublished M.A. thesis, Center for Japanese Studies, University of Michigan.

Blaker, Michael K. (ed.). 1976. Japan at the polls: The House of Councillors election of 1974. Washington, D.C.: American Enterprise Institute for Policy Research.

Curtis, Gerald C. 1971. Election campaigning Japanese style. New York: Columbia University Press.

_____. 1976. "The 1974 election campaign: The political process," in Michael K. Blaker (ed.), Japan at the polls: The House of Councillors election of 1974. Washington, D.C.: American Enterprise Institute for Policy Research.

Kim, Young C. 1967. Political recruitment: The case of Japanese prefectural assemblymen. American Political Science Review, 61:1105-1119.

Miyake Ichirō. 1964. Nihon naikaku no seiji shakaiteki kōsei: Itō naikaku yori Kishi naikaku (Politico-social study of the Japanese Cabinets: From the Itō Cabinet to the Kishi Cabinet). Jimbun Gakuo, 20:213-32.

Nishikawa Toshiyuki. 1974. Newcomers to the House of Representatives of the Japanese Diet, 1946-1969: Patterns of turnover, recruitment, and career development. Unpublished PhD dissertation, Department of Political Science, University of Hawaii.

Richardson, Bradley M. 1974. Political culture of Japan. Berkeley: University of California Press.

Ryang, Key Sun. 1973. Postwar Japanese political leadership: A study of prime ministers. Asian Survey, 13:1010-20.

Shiratori Rei. 1970. Kōhōsha, tosensha no shakaiteki zokusei (Characteristics of the candidates and successful candidates). In Soma Masao (ed.), Nihon no senkyō, Tokyo: Ushio Shuppansha, 1967.

Sugimori, Koji. 1968. Social background of political leadership in Japan. The Developing Economies, 6:487-509.

Youn, Jung-Suk. 1977. Recruitment of political leadership in postwar Japan, 1958-1972. Unpublished Ph.D. dissertation, Department of Political Science, University of Michigan.

THE PERCEPTIONS AND ATTITUDES
OF JAPANESE CANDIDATES
TOWARD ELECTORAL FACTORS

Minoru Yanagihashi

Candidates in a competitive electoral system have to make continual assessments of their election districts if they are to be successful in their political careers. To determine the "pulse" and character of their districts, they acquire essential information through informal conversations with constituents and with community and group leaders. They can also ascertain the attitudes of voters through opinion polls. These activities usually intensify just before an election.

But even after an election, candidates can learn much by going over the campaign. All candidates try to make some kind of realistic appraisal immediately after the election as to what factors contributed to victory or to defeat. To be sure, this postmortem assessment of electoral factors may not be a truly objective analysis, for each candidate comes with his own biases and limited perspective. Nevertheless, what finally emerges from this reflection is the individual candidate's own image of his election district, his own understanding of the electoral forces at work in his district.

An ongoing evaluation of the electoral scene is necessary if a candidate is to be successful in future elections. He would surely want to correct any mistakes he made in the past campaign, and, perhaps based on his past experience, he may want to try a different approach the next time. Therefore, the image a candidate has of his district will directly influence his future campaign strategy and will determine, to a large extent, his behavior during the campaign. However, a candidate's image of his constituent district has implications beyond the arena of electoral politics, for it can explain in part the politician's performance in the legislative chamber, his position on policy issues, and his behavior toward specific groups.

Estimations of his electoral environment will vary widely, of course, with each individual candidate. The variations may be explained in many ways, but the candidate's personality, his party affiliation, the urban or rural nature of his constituency, his incumbency status, and the level of election in which he is involved are surely some of the more important factors to consider. The diverse assessments of candidates, influenced by the above factors, should reveal much about the nature of candidates' perceptions and attitudes toward electoral factors and about the political milieu of districts.

Research Procedures

This study of Japanese candidates' assessments of their electoral environments is based on data obtained through interviews in 1968 with a sample of successful and unsuccessful candidates in Hyogo Prefecture who had run in elections ranging from the National Diet down to local town assemblies.[1] Hyogo Prefecture was chosen as the site for the interviews because it offered a wide variety of socioeconomic characteristics and political milieus. It contains a large metropolitan center, Kobe (population of 1,288,937 in 1970),[2] and an appreciable number of really rural areas. Moreover, all the major types of elections conducted in Japan, including the important metropolitan elections, can be found in Hyogo.

Since it was not possible to interview sufficient numbers of candidates from the entire prefecture, candidates from only two election districts (senkyō-ku) of Hyogo—the First and Fifth—were sampled. The demographic and socioeconomic characteristics and the political climate of the First District differ sharply from those of the Fifth. The First consists of the city of Kobe and is the most urbanized area of the prefecture, whereas the Fifth District includes some of the most rural areas of Hyogo. The First and Fifth Election Districts are constituent units for the national House of Representatives election, but since they are too large as units for local elections, local candidates from subunits within them had to be sampled. For the First District, candidates from Nada-ward (population of 170,791 in 1970) were chosen; for the Fifth District, candidates from the rural city of Toyooka (44,094) and the towns of Kasumi (15, 568) and Tanto (7,181) were selected. It

---

1. The data for this study were gathered while the author was on a Fulbright-Hays Fellowship from the U.S. Office of Education.
2. All census figures cited in this study are from the Bureau of Statistics 1971.

was primarily for analytical purposes that candidates from political units with a wide range of socioeconomic characteristics were selected. Distinctively rural and urban political units were appropriate for comparing candidates operating in quite different environmental contexts and for examining the effects of the environment on the cognitions and attitudes of candidates.

TABLE 1
Composition of the Sample

Level of Election

	Nat.	Pref.	Metro.	Rural City	Town	Total
Urban Candidates						
Conservatives[a]	1	2	5			8
Progressives[b]	3	2	7			12
CGP[c]	1	0	1			2
Rural Candidates						
Conservatives	2	3		10	18	33
Progressives	2	2		4	2	10
CGP[c]	0	0		1	0	1
All-Prefecture						
Conservatives	2	1				3
Progressives	2	1				3
CGP[c]	1	0				1
Total	14	11	13	15	20	73

Notes:
a. Includes candidates of the Liberal Democratic Party (LDP) and independent candidates who acknowledged their conservative leanings.

b. Includes candidates of the Japan Socialist Party (JSP), Democratic Socialist Party (DSP), Japan Communist Party (JCP), and a few independents with progressive leanings.

c. Clean Government Party.

From the above discussion of the choice of election units from Hyogo, it is clear that the approach used to determine the composition of the sample of candidates was to sample the election units and the types of elections rather than to randomly select from a general list of candidates. This procedure provided an even distribution of candidates for each type of election. The types of elections involved were the national Diet elections, the prefectural gubernatorial and assembly elections, the metropolitan or city mayoral and assembly elections, and the town mayoral and assembly elections (see

Table 1). A proportional number of both winning and losing candidates were selected for each of the election categories. Out of a total of 77 candidates chosen, 73 (94.8%) granted interviews, a surprisingly high response rate. Of the four who refused interviews, three were Japan Communist Party candidates running at the national level who declined because of established party policy. At the local levels, however, the noninterview policy was not followed, for three Communist candidates consented to interviews.

The election units studied here were chosen to represent a variety of electoral environments. Moreover, there are no great regional differences in Japan to inhibit generalization at the national level. My own pretests of candidates from other prefectures confirm the impression that, given similar types of socioeconomic environments, candidate responses are consistent nationwide.[3]

Variables

The principal focus of this study is to discover 1) the importance of key electoral factors as seen by the candidates themselves, and 2) how these evaluations are affected by the candidates' differences: their parties, the urban or rural nature of their constituencies, whether or not they are incumbents, and the level of the election. Five electoral factors have been selected for examination. Three pertain to the attitudes of voters: their responses to party labels, policy issues, and individual candidate's personality or image when deciding how to vote.[4] Two are more structural: support groups and "influentials" or "local notables" (yūryokusha). These last two factors have often been identified as crucial in Japan, where social relationships are held to be extremely important.[5] Any Japanese candidate must assess the importance of all five electoral factors when planning (or evaluating) a campaign. We may now see how their assessments differ.

---

3. A pretest of the questionnaire was carried out with candidates in Kanagawa, Saitama, and Tottori prefectures, representing six different types of elections.
4. These three factors have been the center of American research on voting behavior, and are discussed in more detail in the article by Thomas Rochon in this volume.
5. For specific use of these variables in Japanese electoral studies, see Richardson 1974, and Curtis 1971.

Findings

Party Label

Japanese political parties can be placed in a left-to-right continuum, with those on the left, the so-called "progressives," being quite distinct in ideology and policy from those on the right, the "conservatives."[6] Moreover, there are differences in the socioeconomic background of progressives and conservatives, and each side is associated with certain occupational groups. Progressive parties have strong support from blue- and white-collar workers, while the conservative party relies heavily on support from farmers. There are differences by educational level as well, with the better educated tending to support the progressives.

While the distinctiveness of the parties remains, party allegiance as a whole has declined from what it was in the 1950s and 1960s. In the large cities, and especially among young people, the number of independent voters has dramatically increased. There are many reasons for the decline of party appeal, including changes in social networks, weakening of traditional values, and general dissatisfaction with party performance (Ike 1978). Given the apparent decline in the importance to voters of the party label, it is of considerable interest to see how electoral politicians perceived the significance of parties.

Candidates were asked how important their party label was in the election. As can be seen in Table 2, party label was judged to be important by only about one-third of the respondents. This placed party name among the lowest in percentage of importance reported for the five dependent variables analyzed. Considering the large number of rural respondents in the sample, the low saliency of party label was not surprising.

There were clear differences by party affiliation. Only one-fourth of the conservative candidates believed party label was of some importance,

---

6. For analytical purposes, the left-wing progressive parties have been grouped together in this study, but it should be noted that there are differences in the ideologies of these parties. The Japan Communist Party is on the extreme left of the political spectrum. Close to it is the Japan Socialist Party, which has often taken policy stances similar to those of the JCP. The Democratic Socialist Party, on the other hand, is a distinctively moderate socialist party. Although there are significant ideological differences between these parties, they do have basically the same type of support patterns: they all appeal to the working class. Moreover, they have similar organizational structures.

whereas about half of the progressives had strong feelings about the importance of party label for their campaign. But it should be noted that several progressive candidates indicated that party label was important in a negative sense, i.e., it was considered a liability for progressive candidates running in rural districts and was often concealed. As one Toyooka City Assembly candidate replied: "In local elections, it is advantageous if you don't show the party label clearly."

TABLE 2
Relative Importance of Party Label
As Perceived by Candidates

	Degree of Importance				
	Some	Little or No	Don't Know	Total	N
All Candidates	36%	63%	1%	100%	73
Party Affiliation					
Conservatives	24	74	2	100	46
Progressives	52	48	0	100	23
	Gamma = -.46				
Urban-Rural					
Urban	55	41	5	101	22
Rural	18	82	0	100	44
	Gamma = .71				
Incumbency Status					
Incumbents	37	63	0	100	43
Nonincumbents	33	63	4	100	30
	Gamma = .06				
Level of Election					
National	64	36	0	100	14
Prefectural	82	18	0	100	11
Metropolitan	31	62	7	100	13
Local	11	89	0	100	35
	Gamma = .73				

That the environment was of crucial importance in candidates' perceptions is borne out by the big difference between urban and rural candidates. A large majority (82 percent) of rural candidates viewed party to be of little or no importance as compared to only 41 percent of urban candidates. It is well-known that party organization remains feeble and almost nonexistent at the grass-roots level and that rural voters have a low regard for partisanship. An indication of the weak role played by parties in rural areas is the absence of party-affiliated candidates in local town elections. All the candidates running in the towns of Tanto and Kasumi were independents.

Incumbency status had no effect on the candidate's perception of party importance. In contrast, the level of election was a major variable. As expected, a large majority of local candidates believed parties to be of little influence. But at the higher levels, parties are more active and have a greater role to play. It was curious, therefore, that prefectural candidates rated parties much more important than parliamentary candidates did. A closer examination revealed that it was national politicians running in the rural Fifth District who minimized the importance of parties. All four Diet candidates in the district said parties were not important. The respondents probably had in mind the ineffectiveness of the parties as campaign organizations. Parties are of some influence in the formation of political attitudes, but even here they are probably of secondary importance. The incumbent Diet candidate, Arita Kiichi, proudly proclaimed: "It wasn't the LDP that was important; it was Arita's organization!" (He was referring to his kōenkai or personal supporters' association.) Another LDP candidate said: "We're in the countryside, and this has become an individual-type election." Hence, what counts in a rural district is one's own popularity and personality rather than the support of one's party organization.

To summarize, the environmental factors emerged as the key variables in explaining the significance of party label. The urban-rural nature of the constituency and the level of election produced the largest differences.

Issues

Public opinion polls and other surveys have revealed how weak the issue orientation of Japanese voters is when compared, for example, with personality of candidates and party affiliation (Shiratori 1972). Many voters are unaware of election issues, especially when they are abstract and remote. However, when a specific issue affects constituents directly or when it is given extensive coverage by the mass media, issue salience can be heightened. Recently, with the public's broader concern and interest in ecological, housing, traffic, and other urban problems, issues have become increasingly important in Japanese elections (Ike 1978).

It is essential to differentiate between issues and interests. Rural voters are aware of their interests. "Instrumental expectations," that is, what a community or group thinks a candidate will do for them, heavily influence rural voting attitudes (Richardson 1974). But issues which cut across communities and groups are of greater concern in urban districts and have less appeal in rural areas.

TABLE 3
Relative Importance of Issues
As Perceived by Candidates

	Degree of Importance				
	Some	Little or No	Don't Know	Total	N
All Candidates	60%	40%	0%	100%	73
Party Affiliation					
Conservatives	54	46	0	100	46
Progressives	70	30	0	100	23
	Gamma = -.32				
Urban-Rural					
Urban	73	27	0	100	22
Rural	52	48	0	100	44
	Gamma = .42				
Incumbency Status					
Incumbents	63	37	0	100	43
Nonincumbents	57	43	0	100	30
	Gamma = .13				
Level of Election					
National	71	29	0	100	14
Prefectural	64	36	0	100	11
Metropolitan	69	31	0	100	13
Local	51	49	0	100	35
	Gamma = .20				

Table 3 shows that issues were considered important by at least 60 percent of the respondents. There was a clear difference between conservative and progressive candidates. As might be expected, progressive candidates were more conscious and concerned about issues; 70 percent considered them to be of some weight. In contrast, only 54 percent of the conservatives regarded policy issues as vital to their campaign. This difference in attitude toward policy issues reflects the strong ideological commitments of progressive candidates, and their dependence on programmatic appeals to gather votes from the working class. Conservative candidates, on the other hand, preferred to emphasize personal techniques, utilizing social networks and making personal appeals to groups (Yanagihashi 1975).

Progressives have strongly opposed the conservatives on many foreign policy issues, but in domestic policies their differences have not been as serious. Nonetheless, there have been some bitter confrontations, particularly at the national level. At the local level policy debates are usually confined to a small and narrow range of local issues. As Table 3 indicates, policy issues were important for close to three-fourths of the national candidates as compared to about half of the local candidates.

The data also show that issues were more important in urban than in rural districts. Rapid urbanization and the influx of a great number of people have caused massive urban problems which are beyond the control of individuals, groups, or even the community. They must be handled by the government. Urban residents have become more aware of policy issues because of the complexity, variety, and impersonality of urban life. Therefore, policy issues have emerged as a key factor in urban elections.

In contrast to the party label case, the level of election made little difference in candidates' perceptions of the importance of issues. Their party affiliation and the urban or rural nature of the constituency were the main factors.

Personality

Japanese politics has been characterized as a highly personalized process, in which social relationships are unusually important and a premium is placed on the individual character and ability of candidates. Although policy issues are becoming more important, many voters continue to be personality-oriented (Richardson 1974).

We would expect, then, that personality would be perceived as an important variable by a large number of candidates. As clearly indicated in Table 4, candidate's personality was believed to be of some importance by almost 80 percent of those interviewed; this represented the highest percentage scored for all the dependent variables examined in the study. Candidates tended to see themselves as the center of attention.

Conservatives and progressives alike ranked personality high, but it was surprising that progressives would rate personality higher than conservatives. This result was related to the unexpected responses of metropolitan candidates, all of whom ranked personality high, including seven progressive candidates. Interestingly enough, national candidates also rated the personality factor more positively than local candidates. A possible reason is that local assembly candidates often see themselves as pure representatives of their village or neighborhood, requiring little beyond an endorsement to be elected. The heavy response for personality by progressive candidates is interesting in that official pronouncements of the progressive parties often emphasize the importance of policy issues.

TABLE 4
Relative Importance of Personality
As Perceived by Candidates

	Degree of Importance				
	Some	Little or No	Don't Know	Total	N
All Candidates	79%	14%	7%	100%	73
Party Affiliation					
Conservatives	74	15	11	100	46
Progressives	87	13	0	100	23
		Gamma = -.16			
Urban Rural					
Urban	100	0	0	100	22
Rural	68	20	11	99	44
		Gamma = 1.0			
Incumbency Status					
Incumbent	84	11	4	99	43
Nonincumbent	73	17	10	100	30
		Gamma = .24			
Level of Election					
National	93	7	0	100	14
Prefectural	73	27	0	100	11
Metropolitan	100	0	0	100	13
Local	69	17	14	100	35
		Gamma = .22			

Table 4 shows that incumbents and nonincumbents had somewhat different assessments about personality; a greater number of incumbents believed personality aspects to be important than did nonincumbents. Since incumbents had higher recognition, they could stress personality in the campaign. They were constantly in the public's view; they were able to make themselves known among voters by engaging in all kinds of political and social activities; and they were able to expand and strengthen their support by providing patronage and services to constituents and groups. However, it is clear that the urban-rural difference was most important.

Groups

Japan remains today a strongly group-oriented society. In the realm of voting behavior, the importance of group influence has been widely discussed. Groups are able to exert considerable influence on their membership primarily because members tend to put group considerations ahead of their personal needs. The more organized groups, such as labor unions, are frequently affiliated with a political party, tend to be highly politicized at the national level, and are capable of mobilizing their memberships' vote. Even community-type organizations, including the rural burakukai ("hamlet associations") and the urban chōnaikai ("neighborhood associations") are able to exert strong influence on their members.

TABLE 5
Relative Importance of Groups
As Perceived by Candidates

	Degree of Importance				
	Some	Little or No	Don't Know	Total	N
All Candidates	63%	34%	3%	100%	73
Party Affiliation					
Conservatives	52	44	4	100	46
Progressives	83	17	0	100	23
		Gamma = -.60			
Urban-Rural					
Urban	82	14	5	101	22
Rural	55	43	2	100	44
		Gamma = .65			
Incumbency Status					
Incumbent	67	30	3	100	43
Nonincumbent	57	40	3	100	30
		Gamma = .22			
Level of Election					
National	57	36	7	100	14
Prefectural	82	18	0	100	11
Metropolitan	93	0	7	100	13
Local	49	51	0	100	35
		Gamma = .37			

Respondents were asked about the importance of groups in the election. The results are shown in Table 5. Over 60 percent of the candidates believed groups were important in the election. Progressive candidates particularly emphasized groups, with a response of 83 percent. In contrast, only 52 percent of the conservatives rated groups as important electoral factors.

The heavy reliance on groups among progressive candidates can be accounted for by their strong ties with labor unions. Conservatives were not as dependent on organized groups, and they were evenly divided in their opinions about the importance of them. It was evident from comments made by conservative candidates that they were not as enthusiastic as progressives about group support; conservatives generally felt that their group support was not as well organized and consequently not particularly dependable.

Nonincumbents were expected to rely more on organizational support because of their lack of resources and experience, and their inability to generate broad support in the brief period of an election campaign. However, the data showed that nonincumbents relied less on organizational support than incumbents by a small margin. A closer examination of the nonincumbents revealed that there were about twice as many conservatives as progressives, and it was the low regard for support groups by these conservative nonincumbents that depressed the overall percentage for nonincumbents.

It is interesting to note that metropolitan candidates thought groups most important, with 93 percent giving positive responses. A possible explanation is that large urban centers have a multitude of various organizations concentrated within a small area. Many of these are district-type organizations, which are transformed into support groups for candidates during the campaign. Their usual function is to provide social or community services, and they become electoral organizations only when they are mobilized to support the candidacies of their leaders or affiliates. Examples of this type of organization are the Parent-Teacher Association and the various associations for neighborhoods, women, and merchants. Given the availability of these groups, it was not surprising that metropolitan candidates considered them to be a significant electoral factor. Of course, many of these urban candidates were progressives, who, as noted previously, depend mainly on groups for support.

Rural candidates did not feel groups were as important. Nevertheless, they were concerned about changes in the nature of group support occurring in their communities. Respondents in Toyooka, Kasumi, and Tanto were worried that encroaching urbanization was changing the occupational patterns and thus expanding the influence of certain groups. There had been a decrease in those employed in farming and fishing and an increase in those working in profitable nonagricultural occupations in construction, manufacturing, and wholesale and retail trade. By 1970, over 90 percent of the workers in Toyooka, Kasumi, and Tanto were engaged in nonagricultural work to some degree (Bureau of Statistics 1971). Many of these workers had become members of labor unions, trade associations, or other types of groups associated with their place of employment, and rural candidates worried that they had come under the influence of these organizations.

In the analysis of the perceived importance of groups, party affiliation and the urban-rural dimension had the greatest impact. Progressive candidates and those in urban districts had the most need for group support in vote-gathering. Conservative candidates in rural districts, by contrast, had the least need for organizational support and preferred the personalized approach.

Yūryokusha

Yūryokusha, or local influentials, have been mentioned in the literature on Japanese politics as important actors who are able to gather the votes of those who are within their spheres of influence. It is argued that the traditional attitude and behavior of deferring to political authority persist among rural people and among the poor and less educated of the urban population, who are not interested in or informed about politics. On political matters, they find it easier to defer to political bosses or local notables who have social status and the necessary expertise (Steiner 1965; Ikeda 1968). Others have contended, however, that the influence of yūryokusha is questionable and declining (Fukutake 1971). Given the role attributed to influentials, it is of interest to examine how candidates perceived the importance of this factor in their situation.

The results given in Table 6 do not support the notion that yūryokusha are an important means for gathering votes. Only 38 percent of all the candidates considered this factor to be of some importance, the second lowest percentage (after party label) of the dependent variables tested.

It is noteworthy that there was practically no difference between conservative and progressive candidates. This was at variance with the commonly held belief that conservative candidates are much more dependent on local notables to help gather votes. Progressive candidates can rely on labor unions to reach a sizable number of voters, but conservative candidates are said to depend on a more personalized approach involving yūryokusha.

The urban-rural dimension produced the widest difference, but in the opposite to the expected direction. Only about one-third of rural candidates, compared with one-half of the urban candidates, believed influentials to be of some significance. Yūryokusha are supposed to play a vital role in the support patterns of local, prefectural, and national politicians in rural areas, but the data in Table 6 show that the majority of rural candidates felt yūryokusha to be of little or no importance.

TABLE 6
Relative Importance of Yūryokusha
As Perceived by Candidates

	Degree of Importance				
	Some	Little or No	Don't Know	Total	N
All Candidates	38%	59%	3%	100%	73
Party Affiliation					
Conservatives	39	61	0	100	46
Progressives	39	52	9	100	23
	Gamma = −.08				
Urban-Rural					
Urban	55	36	9	100	22
Rural	32	68	0	100	44
	Gamma = .53				
Incumbency Status					
Incumbent	30	67	3	100	43
Nonincumbents	50	47	3	100	30
	Gamma = −.07				
Level of Election					
National	29	64	7	100	14
Prefectural	27	73	0	100	11
Metropolitan	62	31	7	100	13
Local	37	63	0	100	35
	Gamma = .05				

An explanation for the above discrepancy could lie with a definitional problem. Yūryokusha can be defined in a number of ways. In its strictest sense, it is limited to local notables or influentials, frequently from former prominent landholding families, who used to monopolize leadership positions in their communities. Rural candidates, by using this narrow definition, may have excluded rising new groups of elites, many of whom are entrepreneurs who have established small businesses, or are owners of other commercial enterprises, or are elected office holders. Such groups have replaced the traditional elites from landholding families.

The high regard for yūryokusha among urban candidates, particularly those contesting metropolitan elections, is equally surprising.[7] Again the difficulty may well be definitional. Urban respondents seem to have had a broader definition of yūryokusha in mind, including within this term business-

---

7. The diminished influence of city ward yūryokusha was already evident in the early 1950s. See Dore 1958:282-83.

men and other community leaders. Conflicting definitions may thus explain these unexpected findings, but further research is needed to clarify the role of influentials in the urban and rural contexts.

Although the differences are relatively small, it is interesting that more nonincumbents considered yūryokusha to be significant than did incumbents. This reliance upon local notables may be directly related to the lack of resources and experience among nonincumbents. They do not have the time to establish a strong network of personal supporters or to win over the electorate. Consequently, nonincumbents may seek the help of available yūryokusha.

Today the political influence of the yūryokusha is not what it was a couple of decades ago. Although respondents indicated that local influentials do not have the vote-mobilizing power they were once assumed to have in their districts, they were cited for their continued importance in the nomination of candidates and in the supplying of financial support. An upper house candidate had this to say about the present role of the yūryokusha: "In financial matters, yūryokusha have a very important role, but they continue to be weakened in their ability to gather votes in outlying areas." Accordingly, it seems that local influentials have lost a major part of their power, their vote-mobilization abilities.

Attitudes Toward Voters

Our finding that, in general, conservatives and progressives had remarkably similar attitudes and perceptions toward electoral factors is interesting. To probe this similarity of views more extensively, candidates were asked about voters' interest in and knowledge about elections. The results are

TABLE 7
Voters' Political Awareness As Perceived by
Conservative and Progressive Candidates

	Some	Little or None	Don't Know	Total	N
Are Voters Interested?					
Conservatives	82%	17%	0%	99%	46
Progressives	78	22	0	100	23
		Gamma = .14			
Are Voters Informed?					
Conservatives	63	33	4	100	46
Progressives	56	39	4	99	23
		Gamma = .15			

presented in Table 7. Both sides had favorable impressions about the interest of voters, with approximately 80 percent of the conservatives and of the progressives believing voters had at least some interest in the election. On the question of voters' competency, there was a negligible difference between the two: conservative and progressive candidates agreed that voters were relatively poorly informed.

Implications

The polarization of political parties has been emphasized in much of the literature on Japanese politics. The deep programmatic differences between the ruling conservative party and the progressive opposition, with a resulting lack of dialogue, continuing distrust over legislative proceedings, and bitter splits over policy issues, have been discussed at length.

The programmatic differences between the conservative and progressive parties are largely the result of their disparate ideological positions and support patterns. As far as organizational structure and leadership patterns are concerned, however, there are few differences between the camps. Of all major political parties, only the Clean Government Party and the JCP are mass organizations with grass-roots strength, and only the CGP can be said to be free from intraparty factionalism. Although JSP factions are based on ideological considerations, they remain cliques built around personal loyalties and in this sense are similar to factions in the LDP.

In view of the often-stated differences between the conservative and progressive parties, and the confrontations that have resulted from these differences, we expected conservative and progressive candidates to have different opinions about electoral factors. Therefore, it was surprising to find striking similarities in the attitudes of conservative and progressive candidates with regard to most of the factors studied.

What accounts for this convergence? One explanation can be found in the basic preference for personal appeals among most Japanese. Programmatic appeals may be increasing in importance, but electoral politicians continue to believe that personal appeals have the greatest impact. Even progressive parties find that they must resort to such appeals in broadening their base of support. It is in program and ideology that the two sides differ the most, but it is precisely these aspects which have been underplayed in order to broaden the appeal of the parties.

Another perhaps more basic explanation is the persistence of parochial attitudes among voters. Two in particular were frequently mentioned in interviews, especially by candidates in local-level elections: mijika and jimoto. Roughly translated, mijika means "close to oneself" and jimoto "local district." Both are similar to what V. O. Key called the "friends and neighbors" effect in southern United States politics (Key 1949:37-41). Mijika results in a tendency to be most concerned about the candidates that are physically and cognitively closest—the local rather than the prefectural or national candidate, the candidate for the assembly rather than for mayor or governor. The local assemblyman, after all, may live around the corner. Jimoto refers to the strong emotional feelings of local inhabitants for their community or district. Citizens are expected to turn out and support the hometown candidate. Voters feel intimate with their local candidate and have a strong sense of loyalty toward him, based on community ties that override other concerns.

Thus, the traditional sentiments of mijika and jimoto deemphasize programmatic appeals and partisan politics and instead promote a convergence of views that is highly parochial. Our findings indicate that candidates' attitudes mainly reflected the prevailing sentiments of their electoral environments. Undoubtedly these traditional sentiments, strongest in the more rural areas, contributed to the similarity in the attitudes of conservative and progressive candidates.

Another case of little difference in attitudes is between incumbents and challengers. Considering the differences in the resources available to them and the differences in experience and knowledge they bring to the electoral contest, one would expect fundamental differences in perceptions of the electoral environment. Our data reveal that while incumbents and nonincumbents did differ slightly in their assessments of some electoral factors, the similarities are much more impressive.

The similarities we found in the attitudes and perceptions of candidates have important implications for the stability of the electoral system. They may very well account for the remarkable smoothness with which the electoral process has operated in postwar years. An exceptional case in all of Asia, Japan has held regular elections without serious disruptions and violence. Japanese candidates—progressives and conservatives, winners as well as losers, incumbents as well as nonincumbents—have come to accept the "rules of the electoral game." All have accommodated to the competition for votes, the numerous and stringent regulations governing campaigns, and a very complex system of elections. To be sure, detailed electoral regulations have been widely abused out of sheer necessity, and there have been complaints about the system of elections, particularly the nature of the multi-member districts and the problem of malapportionment. But few electoral politicians have seriously advocated full-scale changes for fear they would eventually affect their own vested interests and take away any advantages presently enjoyed. Thus, most electoral politicians accept the "system" and seek to operate within its framework.

The legislative arena, in contrast, has seen much greater disruption. Progressives have on occasion been advocates of "parliamentarism-plus," that is, the willingness to go beyond parliamentary government in order to achieve one's objectives. Specifically, the use of demonstrations, sitdowns, street violence, and other obstructional tactics are considered legitimate (Scalapino and Masumi 1962). The ruling conservatives, on their part, have at times provoked the opposition by ignoring their views and ramming through bills with underhanded and questionable tactics, thus showing their utter distrust of the opposition at crucial moments. In these crisis situations, the foundations of parliamentarism in Japan have been visibly shaken (Baerwald 1970).[8]

The findings indicate how well candidates have adapted themselves to their electoral environment. This successful adaptation may be a factor contributing to the stability of the electoral process. Regardless of the ideological pronouncements of parties, the myriad sources of support, or even differences in the experiences and resources possessed by candidates, the competition for elective office seems to engender and foster a commonality of views about the electoral process among participants. This similarity of views transcends marked differences that divide the parties along ideological and support lines.

Our findings revealed that the urban-rural nature of the constituency was the most powerful and consistent variable in explaining differences in candidates' views. In the analysis of the dependent variables of party label, issues, personality, groups, and yūryokusha, rural candidates were found to perceive *all* of them as less important. The differences between rural and urban candidates in all these variables were quite significant (see Table 8).

---

8. However, since the decline of the LDP's Diet majority in the mid-1970s, a greater degree of shared orientation and less frequent recourse to disruptive tactics have come to characterize the legislative arena as well.

TABLE 8
Summary: Effects on Perceived Electoral Factors[a]

Dependent Variables	Independent Variables			
	Party Affiliation	Urban-Rural	Incumbency	Level of Election
Party Label	-.46	.71	.06	.73
Issues	-.32	.42	.13	.20
Personality	-.16	1.00	.24	.22
Groups	-.60	.65	.22	.37
Yūryokusha	-.08	.53	-.07	.05

Note:
a. All correlations are gammas.

Although urbanization has taken place rapidly, and economic forces and the mass media have penetrated rural areas, the style of politics has changed remarkably little, at least insofar as local-level candidates in more rural areas are concerned. However, these trends have had serious consequences for national politicians. The affective ties that Japanese voters have with their candidates tend to disappear in higher-level elections as candidates represent larger constituencies and traditional jimoto sentiments are weakened. Moreover, mijika deteriorates as issues become remote and voters lose their sense of connection with candidates, for not only are candidates more distant, but there are more of them.

It is at the point when traditional community sentiments and affective ties with candidates are weakened that other forces are likely to influence voters' decisions. Competing political parties and groups are now able to take advantage of the weakened relationship between conservative supporters and higher-level politicians and thus make inroads into conservative strength. The intrusion of other actors has quickened the demise of the yūryokusha. Influentials find it more and more difficult to control votes for higher-level candidates, especially votes from peripheral areas in their districts. They continue to have close relationships with higher-level politicians and to promise delivery of votes, but they can no longer guarantee a solid bloc of votes. Many Diet candidates have turned to other actors to help mobilize votes; indeed, Diet candidates have developed alternate means of securing grass-roots support because of the unreliability of the yūryokusha.

What emerges from this study as the most important independent variable in explaining candidates' perceptions and attitudes is the urban-rural dimension. Neither the ideological background, nor the base of support of party affiliation, nor the experiences and resources possessed by candidates, affected perceptions and attitudes as much as this environmental factor. Since the nature of the electoral environment is so important, one could speculate that changes in it resulting from increasing urbanization will result in a convergence of views about electoral factors. But this will be true only if parties and political expertise remain relatively insignificant in local elections, and this development, in turn, is dependent upon the degree to which traditional attitudes and patterns of behavior persist in the rural areas. To date, the pattern of development has been the persistence of traditional attitudes and behavior and the insignificance of partisan politics at local levels. This is probably the principal reason why the attitudinal structures of candidates have been basically alike. Once traditional sentiments and patterns are weakened to an extent where they are no longer an important influence, party affiliation and incumbency status would probably become important and would replace the urban-rural dimension as the critical factor influencing perceptions and attitudes of candidates. If and when such a development fully takes place, there will be differences in the attitudes and behavior of candidates by party affiliation, that is, conservatives will clearly differ from progressives. There will then be a divergence rather than a convergence of political attitudes and views. But the likelihood of such a development seems remote for some time to come.

References

Baerwald, Hans H. 1970. An aspect of Japanese parliamentary politics. The Japan Interpreter, 6:196-205.

Bureau of Statistics (Japan). 1971. 1970 population census of Japan, Vol. 3. Tokyo: Ministry of Finance Printing Office.

Curtis, Gerald L. 1971. Election campaigning Japanese style. New York: Columbia University Press.

Dore, R.P. 1958. City life in Japan: A study of a Tokyo ward. Berkeley: University of California Press.

Fukutake Tadashi. 1971. Nihon no nōson (Japanese farm villages). Tokyo: Tokyo Daigaku Shuppankai.

Ike, Nobutaka. 1978. A theory of Japanese democracy. Boulder, Colorado: Westview Press.

Ikeda, George K. 1968. Ishikawa--electoral politics in a Japanese prefecture. Unpublished Ph.D. dissertation, Department of Government, Harvard University.

Key, V.O., Jr. 1949. Southern politics in state and nation. New York: Alfred A. Knopf.

Richardson, Bradley M. 1974. The political culture of Japan. Berkeley: University of California Press.

Scalapino, Robert A., and Junnosuke Masumi. 1962. Parties and politics in contemporary Japan. Berkeley: University of California Press.

Shiratori Rei. 1972. Seron, senkyō, seiji: kawaru Nihonjin no seiji ishiki (Public opinion, elections, politics: Changing Japanese political consciousness). Tokyo: Nihon Keizai Shimbunsha.

Steiner, Kurt. 1965. Local government in Japan. Stanford: Stanford University Press.

Yanagihashi, Minoru. 1975. Electoral politics in contemporary Japan: candidates in different levels and types of elections in Hyogo prefecture. Unpublished Ph.D. dissertation, Department of Political Science, University of Michigan.

GUBERNATORIAL ELECTIONS IN JAPAN

Steven R. Reed

A primary goal of the American Occupation was to democratize Japanese politics by creating local autonomy. Autonomous and democratized local governments were to become the "schoolhouses of democracy" and serve as a barrier to any return to militarism. One of the key institutional reforms in pursuit of local autonomy and democracy was to make the position of prefectural governor elective. Before the war, governors had been Ministry of Home Affairs (MOHA) officials and these appointed bureaucrats played a pivotal role in maintaining a high level of centralization. (See Steiner 1965 and Takaki 1974.) It would seem, therefore, that Occupation officials chose a good position to democratize to produce new faces and vigorous grassroots competition. Yet, the conclusion reached by students of Japan after the war was that the effort to create local autonomy had failed and that centralization persisted. (Steiner 1965; virtually all Japanese specialists would strongly support this conclusion.)

One indication of this failure to produce local autonomy came in the first gubernatorial elections of 1947. The electorates of 24 of the 46 prefectures chose to retain their appointed governors and four more successful candidates had been appointed governors previously or in other prefectures (Steiner 1965:445). Even after 1947, incumbents and candidates with bureaucratic backgrounds continued to dominate gubernatorial elections. Data on 218 gubernatorial elections in the postwar period yield a success rate of 89 percent for incumbents. Data on the backgrounds of governors are less readily available, but in 1965, 65 percent of the governors had had bureaucratic careers (Kim 1968).

The hope and expectations that gubernatorial elections would produce vigorous and competitive contests were also dashed by experience. Issue-oriented elections offering the voters a real choice between a conservative and a progressive candidate proved a rare occurrence. Several progressive governors were elected in the immediate postwar period, but, with the notable exception of Governor Ninagawa of Kyoto, they proved short-lived. Gubernatorial elections were dominated by conservatives. Of the 108 governors I was able to classify, 86 (80 percent) were conservative and only 9 were progressive. The remaining 13 governors were middle-of-the-road, supported by both conservatives and one or more progressive parties.

The advantages of incumbency and the weakness of progressive candidates produced many non-competitive elections. Such elections, including both uncontested elections and contests in which the only opposition came from token Communist or other minor party candidates, comprise 31 percent of the 324 elections for which I have data. If we exclude those formally competitive elections in which the winning candidate received over twice the vote of his nearest rival, only 51 percent of these 324 were truly competitive.

Even many of these "competitive" elections were not issue-oriented, conservative versus progressive contests, but internecine battles among conservative parties or factions. From 1947 to 1955, competition between the conservative Liberal and Democratic Parties had often provided voters with a choice of candidates, if not necessarily a choice between different issue positions. In 1955, the two conservative parties merged into the Liberal Democratic Party (LDP). Although the merger did not proceed smoothly in all prefectures, the combination of the two conservative parties held large majorities in most prefectures, and prefectural politics tended to revolve around the normally issueless factional politics within the LDP.[1] The question of who should be chairman of the assembly, a relatively powerless position, often produced major political controversy. Occasionally the LDP would split over the choice of a gubernatorial candidate, allowing a progressive candidate to win if he could unite most of the progressive parties behind his candidacy, but such victories required extraordinary circumstances.

The LDP's economic policy of promoting industrial development helped consolidate conservative dominance by creating central government largess in the form of central grants to be distributed by LDP politicians. The proposition that the LDP would discriminate against opposition-controlled

---

1. Conservative factional politics is usually described as issueless and often is. However, I have seen several indications that real issues were involved in the factional politics of the high-growth era. The LDP is a party of business and agriculture, and the two are not always in harmony. In the history of Chiba Prefecture, at least, factions sometimes represented either industrialization first and foremost or industrialization to aid agriculture. The codeword for greater emphasis on agriculture was "balanced growth."

localities seemed so commonsensical that some progressive mayors even switched to the LDP to enhance their chances for grants, though there is little evidence to indicate that such discrimination actually took place.[2] The LDP did manage to take political credit for both national and regional economic growth. Moreover, during this period progressive parties at the local level did not oppose the LDP's economic policies or develop alternative programs, again with the exception of Governor Ninagawa.[3]

The reform of making governors elective did not live up to expectations; it did not seem to contribute to local autonomy or local democracy. However, beginning in the late 1960s, a new generation of progressive mayors and governors was elected, and their election, policies, and popularity promised fulfillment of postwar hopes and expectations. Voters were more often offered a choice between a conservative and a progressive candidate. Progressive parties found it easier to unite behind a single candidate when the prospects for victory looked good. The progressives also found issues behind which they could unite: pollution control, citizen participation, and welfare. Local governments headed by progressive mayors and governors initiated innovative policies that played a key role in turning Japanese government from a singleminded pursuit of economic growth toward "quality of life" issues.[4] The outlook for both local automony and local democracy looked bright. One could reasonably argue that the Occupation reforms had not failed; it had merely taken time for institutional changes to produce behavioral results.

The accomplishments of this period cannot be denied, but many commentators are suggesting that this era of local autonomy is already over. In the gubernatorial elections of 1978 and 1979, conservatives regained several seats and progressives won no new ones (<u>Nihon Keizai Shimbun</u> 1979b). In particular, the three "stars" of the progressive camp, Ninagawa of Kyoto, Minobe of Tokyo, and Mayor Asukata of Yokohama City, who had been

---

2. Some evidence that there was not much discrimination against local governments based on their political complexion is contained in my dissertation (Reed 1980).
3. Governor Ninagawa favored development by small rather than large enterprises and development that would create more even distribution of wealth rather than the economically rational policy of concentrating on the most developed areas (The Kyoto Prefectural Administrative Study Group 1973).
4. On the election of these progressive governors and their policies, see Takayose 1975; Toyama 1975; McKean 1977; and MacDougall 1976. Taketsugu Tsurutani interprets these events in terms of the postindustrial society in his <u>Political Change in Japan,</u> 1977.

the leaders in innovative policy making, all retired from public office and were replaced by conservatives. What had seemed bastions of progressive strength were overturned. Some have argued that the conservatives have coopted the issues of the seventies, that the progressives have reverted to disunity and sterile opposition, and that Japan has returned to politics as usual (Nihon Keizai Shimbun 1979b).[5]

Is the "era" of local autonomy over? Has Japan returned to politics as usual? I will address these questions using both case study and quantitative evidence. I collected a variety of case study and anecdotal evidence while doing research in Japan during 1975-76, and have supplemented this evidence with the Japanese literature on the topic.[6] I have also collected quantitative data on gubernatorial elections from a variety of sources.[7] The data set contains bothersome gaps, but covers virtually all the elections from 1950 through 1975 and most thereafter.

The primary goal of this paper is to explain the changing fortunes of progressive candidates. Before we can address these questions, however, we must examine the context of gubernatorial elections in Japan. The second section will describe nomination politics, asking why bureaucratic candidates have been so successful. The third section will deal with patterns of gubernatorial elections, dealing with the advantages of incumbency, the incidence of noncompetitive elections, and the determinants of a candidate's vote. In the fourth section we will return to an analysis of the trends over time, asking how much the patterns have changed and when the turning points occurred.

Nomination Politics

At any given time, most governors have had bureaucratic backgrounds. In 1947, 28 (61 percent) of the governors were ex-MOHA bureaucrats and other successful candidates may have come from other ministries. In 1965, 30 (65 percent) of the governors had had bureaucratic experience (Kim

---

5. A more thorough and strongly argued case can be found in Kaminogō 1978.
6. My research was supported by the United States Educational Commission in Japan (Fulbright Commission) and the Social Science Research Council.
7. The data are drawn primarily from the Senkyō Nenkan (Elections yearbooks) published by the MOHA and the newspapers, but bits and pieces of information have been added whenever I have run across them. Categorizations of party support come from newpapers and Zenkoku Shichō Meibō, 1975.

1968). In 1979, before the April elections, the figure was 26 (57 percent), and it rose to 31 (67 percent) after those elections (Nihon Keizai Shimbun 1979a,c). Although there may be trends hidden among these four time points, these data indicate that the predominance of ex-bureaucrats has been a constant feature of gubernatorial elections. The only clear difference observable in these limited data is the increase in local (normally prefectural) bureaucrats: from one in 1965 to eight in 1979. In 1965, only two other career patterns produced more than one governor. The Diet produced 15 (33 percent), but since six of these also had a bureaucratic background, only 9 (20 percent) had purely legislative careers. Five (11 percent) of the 1965 governors had been mayors (Kim 1968).

Why are so many governors ex-bureaucrats? Why have so few had purely political careers? Part of the answer lies in the image of what a governor should be. As the chief administrative official of the prefecture, a governor is expected to be a cut above the average politician. In terms of prestige, he ranks above an ordinary Dietman and far above a prefectural assemblyman. A governor should be "a man of real ability" (jitsuryokusha). A governor should not only be more able than the average politician, he should be a different type of politician. Prefectural assemblymen and Dietmen are expected to play partisan and factional politics and to represent their constituencies' parochial interests, but a governor should be "above politics" and represent the whole prefecture. The ideal of nonpartisan local government is strong in Japan, and the infusion of American ideas after the war perhaps reinforced this ideal.

In Japanese society and politics, one of the best ways to prove "real ability" and to lay claim to being "above politics" is through a bureaucratic career. The great prestige of a bureaucratic career in Japan means that the bureaucracy attracts many graduates from the best universities, and a bureaucratic career is often taken as evidence of ability. In fact, in my reading of Japanese newspapers, I have yet to see the term jitsuryokusha applied to anyone who lacks a bureaucratic background. The bureaucracy's reputation for honesty and objectivity also enhances an ex-bureaucrat's claim to being "above politics," particularly in contrast to the general belief that politicians are likely to be involved in corruption. Finally, the governor is the chief administrative official of the prefecture, and administrative experience would be a relevant recruitment criterion in any culture. Thus, it is not only proper, but also desirable, to have an ex-bureaucrat in the governor's chair. While I cannot document a preference for bureaucratic candidates among the electorate, the selectorates that choose gubernatorial candidates and the mass media do display such a preference.

Whether or not candidates with bureaucratic backgrounds have an advantage in elections because of their qualifications and image, they have a real advantage in nomination politics. The general desirability of being "above politics" becomes in nomination politics the virtual requirement that the candidate be acceptable to all factions (for a conservative candidate) or all supporting parties (for a progressive candidate). Given the factionalism of the LDP and the fragmentation of the progressives, a candidate must be above politics in the sense of representing more than one faction or party; he must be an "outsider," someone separated from the history of partisan and factional conflict in the prefecture. Ex-bureaucrats are simply the most available and most clearly qualified type of "outsider" candidate.

I was surprised to learn that parties often have great difficulty finding candidates for the post of prefectural governor. The prefectural assembly would seem to be a natural recruiting ground, but the gap in prestige and presumed ability between an assemblyman and a governor is too wide to be bridged often. An assemblyman seldom has the opportunity to develop a prefecture-wide support base, having proven his ability to win elections only with a much smaller electorate. Finally, an assemblyman is almost certain to be closely identified with one faction of the LDP or to one of the local progressive parties. In 1965, only one governor had been an assemblyman immediately before his election (Kim 1968). To give one specific example, in Chiba Prefecture (for which I have nearly complete data) only once was an assemblyman seriously considered for the nomination during the entire postwar period.[8]

Many potential candidates with sufficient stature normally have a desirable position already, as a Dietman or possibly a mayor. Though the governorship would be a step up, these potential candidates would have to risk their present position in order to run. They may also be identified with a particular local faction or party.[9] Sometimes a prefecture experiences a period of consensus which enables a local politician of stature to become governor. Sometimes a Dietman (particularly a member of the House of Councillors which is also supposed to be "above politics") may have sufficient

---

8. The data on Chiba Prefecture come from the Chiba Nippo; from the Tokyo University Social Science Group 1965; from the Chiba Prefecture Citizens' Movement Liaison Council 1975; and from Ohara and Yokoyama 1965.
9. The interconnections among prefectural factions and Dietmen from the prefecture is complex and unstudied. Prefectural newspapers often name the prefectural factions by the Dietmen they presumably support, but the nature of the relationship is unclear.

distance from prefectural politics to play the role of an "outsider," but the pool of potential candidates among politicians is remarkably small.

Where, then, can one find qualified and available candidates? There is one obvious place to look: the vice-governor. The vice-governor is appointed by the governor and is often a central bureaucrat on leave to the prefectural government. No one is more clearly qualified or better trained for the job. Since the vice-governor post is the peak of a prefectural bureaucrat's career and may well be the peak of a central bureaucrat's career, he tends to be available to run. Especially when the need for an election comes up unexpectedly, as when a governor dies in office, all parties are likely to look first to the vice-governor. This was the case in Chiba in 1963. Similarly in Yokohama City when Mayor Asukata resigned all the parties found themselves supporting the vice-mayor. Often vice-governors are able to lay claim to being the legitimate heir to the previous governor and run with some of the advantages of incumbency.

Because the vice-governor is an obvious future gubernatorial candidate, the appointment of a vice-governor can become a partisan or factional issue. Progressive governors often have trouble finding a nominee acceptable to their conservative-dominated assemblies.[10] In this process, central bureaucrats have the advantage of being outsiders, good compromise candidates. However, once appointed, the vice-governor must deal with the assembly regularly. Although if he has political ambitions, he will try to maintain an image of being above partisan politics, the need to develop support in the assembly may lead him to become too closely identified with one faction to gain the necessary broad support. If the vice-governor is disqualified for this or another reason, a department head (often a posted central bureaucrat as well) might well be a logical choice. Thus, in 1965, 14 governors had been either vice-governors or department heads, and, although my data are incomplete for 1979, at least 11 governors had been vice-governors. If no qualified department head can be found, the parties may have to look for a compromise candidate in the central bureaucracy (usually someone born in the prefecture but who has been living in Tokyo for many years). This route provides the main entry for ex-bureaucrats from ministries other than the MOHA, which dominates the major department heads' and vice-governors' positions.

---

10. In larger perfectures, two vice-governors are often appointed, for both administrative and political reasons.

Prefectural politics seldom involve great issues but are often characterized by high levels of conflict. Politics can be divorced from policy. The conflict may be over the "who" rather than the "what" of politics, but it develops a momentum of its own. The more rancorous prefectural politics become, the more likely it is that politicians at all levels will be drawn into the fray, disqualifying them from the outsider role and increasing the need for an uninvolved gubernatorial candidate. Moreover, the more rancorous prefectural politics become, the more likely it is that central bureaucrats will fill the positions of the major department heads, of the vice-governor, and then finally of the governor.

The need to find an outside compromise candidate applies to both conservatives and progressives, but particularly to the latter. Conservative factions do engage in bitter conflicts which periodically split the party, but they are after all factions within a single party. Progressives are divided into parties (as well as intraparty factions), and it is more difficult to unite parties behind a single candidate than to unite factions. Japanese commentators are fond of pointing out that few, if any, of the progressive governors are "truly progressive." Progressive governors cannot be party ideologues and are seldom even party members. Thus, Governor Ninagawa of Kyoto was a disgruntled central bureaucrat before becoming a progressive governor. In the late 1960s academia proved a valuable recruiting ground for the progressive parties, providing Governor Minobe of Tokyo, Governor Nagasu of Kanagawa, Governor Kuroda of Osaka, and Governor Tsunematsu of Shimane. These represent a different type of outsider, but they are outsiders nevertheless. Even when the governor is a party member, commentators question his progressive credentials. Governor Hata of Saitama was a Japan Socialist Party (JSP) member of the House of Councillors before being elected governor, but he belonged to the moderate wing of the party, receives votes from the conservative farmers near his home town, and manages to obtain the cooperation of several conservative assemblymen and mayors. The commentators emphasize these latter factors over his party membership.

The commentators are even more dubious of progressive governors who come from the bureaucracy. Ex-MOHA bureacrats have been elected on the progressive ticket in Okayama and Shiga Prefectures, and at least one more was a serious but unsuccessful candidate in Chiba Prefecture. The 1975 Chiba race saw an ex-MOHA bureaucrat on each side, the conservative vice-governor versus the progressive superintendent of education (kyōiku-chō). The local newspaper congratulated the citizens of Chiba on having a choice between two jitsuryokusha (Chiba Nippo 1975). The superintendent of education had developed some progressive credentials by mediating a bitter conflict between the board of education and the prefectural teachers' unions and by implementing a relatively progressive reform of the high school entrance system, but he was not an idealogue or a party activist. This was the first time Chiba's progressive parties had managed to unite behind a single candidate; that they were able to do so was in large part because of the availability of a good "outsider."

These observations raise the question of what makes a governor progressive. Looking over all the cases, we find a tremendous range of ideas and ideologies. (The same could be said of conservative governors.) Because progressive governors must be outsiders, one can predict very little about the individual simply by knowing he is a progressive. The common denominator is the support of progressive parties. In order to get the support of these parties, a candidate needs some sort of progressive credentials, but one can say little more. However, even if one can predict little about individual progressive candidates, one should still be able to predict some things about the policies a progressive governor will pursue. The cooperation of the progressive parties is usually predicated on a written agreement on the campaign platform among the parties and with the candidate. Moveover, the progressive parties and progressive interest groups should have access to the governor after he is elected. In particular, one can predict that under a progressive governor, the union of local government employees (Jichirō) and the teachers' unions should have a greater voice in policy making. These predictions should hold equally for all progressive governors whether they are ex-bureaucrats, ex-academics, or party members.

The election of a progressive governor does not mean that the workers have risen up to overthrow the oppressors and their corrupt politics, as many progressive parties would like and as many commentators seem to expect it to mean. The election of a progressive governor may be a fluke: the conservatives being so badly split that the progressive can sneak in with a little more than a third of the vote. When the election is not a fluke—when a progressive wins a head-on battle with a conservative—the determining factors are likely to be the attractiveness of the candidates plus a few specific issues. In the late 1960s, progressives ran on a platform of pollution control, slower growth, more welfare, and greater citizen participation. These issues proved effective not only in winning votes, but in attracting good candidates and providing the nucleus around which all progressive parties could unite. Given unity, a good candidate, a couple of issues, and either a split in the LDP or a reasonable balance between the two camps, the progressives have a chance to win the governor's chair. The price of winning, however, includes putting up an outsider candidate with a lowest-common-denominator platform that all supporting parties can accept. But, whether or not these outsiders are "truly progressive," they have done much to change Japanese politics and policies.

In sum, gubernatorial candidates must be acceptable to all factions for a conservative, or all parties for a progressive; they must be compromise candidates, and usually outsiders. The greater the level of conflict in the prefecture, the greater the need for outsider candidates. The predominance of ex-bureaucrats can be explained by their separation from factional and partisan politics and by their relative availability to run. Outsiders are more important to progressives, and they too find willing candidates among ex-bureaucrats. It is this logic in prefectural politics, rather than some conscious design of the central bureaucracy to control local governments, that explains the large number of ex-bureaucrats among governors.

Electoral Patterns

The first point to make about gubernatorial elections is that incumbents are normally reelected. My data yield a success rate of 89% for incumbents. Unless an incumbent seems particularly vulnerable for some reason, the opposition will have a hard time finding a qualified candidate to run and may not even put up a token candidate. The Japan Communist Party (JCP) usually fields a candidate, using the electoral process as an opportunity to "educate" the public, but the outcome of such elections is not in doubt. The adversarial aspects of prefectural politics seldom affect gubernatorial elections when the incumbent runs for another term. Since the incumbent is virtually guaranteed renomination, the nomination process tends to be quiet on one side at least. The power of incumbency is such that the requirement of unity among supporting factions and parties can be waived. Indeed, progressive governors have often survived the defection of part of their support group, most notably in the 1958 election in Kyoto when Governor Ninagawa survived the defection of the JCP. (See the Kyoto Prefectural Administration Study Group 1973.)

Governors can often hold their seats for as long as they wish and many hold on for a long time. Table 1 displays the number of terms served by the 108 governors for whom we have sufficient data. Eleven governors served only one term, but most of these cases occurred early in the postwar period; several of the governors elected in 1947 retired after one term, and some prefectures, notably Kochi and Miyazaki, experienced two or three one-term governors before settling down to a normal pattern. The early volatility may be attributed to the generally unsettled nature of the immediate postwar period and unfamiliarity with the system of electing governors. Normally, governors serve at least two terms; some last for over twenty years. The distribution of terms is about the same for conservative, progressive, and middle-of-the-road governors. The somewhat larger number of short-term conservatives is largely due to the fact that they were dominant during the early volatile period and later subject to some dislocations occasioned by the formation of the LDP in 1955.

TABLE 1
Terms Served by Governors

Terms	Conservatives		Middle-of-the-road		Progressives		Total	
1	10.5%	(9)	7.7%	(1)	11.1%	(1)	10.2%	(11)
2	39.5	(34)	30.8	(4)	11.1	(1)	6.1	(39)
3	23.3	(20)	30.8	(4)	55.6	(5)	26.9	(29)
4	11.6	(10)	23.1	(3)	0.0		12.0	(13)
5	8.1	(7)	7.7	(1)	11.1	(1)	8.3	(9)
6	5.8	(5)	0.0		0.0		4.6	(5)
7	1.2	(1)	0.0		11.1	(1)	1.9	(2)
Total	100.0%	(86)	100.0%	(13)	100.0%	(9)	100.0%	(108)

Note: Numbers in parentheses are the absolute numbers. Governors still in office were counted when they had served three or more terms, so the percentages of those serving many terms is somewhat underestimated. To have excluded these cases, however, would have greatly biased the results toward short careers. The coding of the governor's political support is based on several sources. I coded middle-of-the-road candidates as those who received the support of one conservative party (the Liberals, the Democrats, or the LDP) and a progressive party. Progressives are defined as those supported only by progressive parties. The first election is taken as definitive; incumbents often get very broad support.

TABLE 2
Distribution of Defeated Incumbents

Term	Conservatives	Middle-of-the-Road	Progressives	All	N	Success Rate
2	6	1	0	7	116	94.0%
3	11	0	2	13	68	80.9
4	2	1	0	3	32	90.6
5	1	1	0	2	18	88.9
6	0	0	0	0	7	100.0
7	1	0	0	1	3	66.7
Total	21	3	2	26	244	89.3%

Note: See note to Table 1. The "term" is that being contested, e.g., the 2 row represents incumbents who have completed one term in office. The "N" is the total number of elections contested by incumbents.

TABLE 3
Winning Percentages by Number
of Terms and Party Support

Term	All	Conservatives	Middle-of-the-Road	Progressives
1	59.4 (115)	61.2 (79)	56.5 (23)	53.7 (13)
2	72.4 (111)	71.8 (85)	80.5 (17)	63.2 (9)
3	67.8 (67)	64.8 (49)	79.9 (11)	69.3 (7)
4	68.2 (32)	67.5 (22)	68.4 (8)	74.2 (2)
5	62.2 (18)	62.3 (13)	64.5 (3)	58.1 (1)
6	57.4 (6)	57.7 (5)		56.2 (1)
7	47.4 (2)	47.4 (2)		

Note: Numbers in parentheses are the respective N's. The N includes all winners and all incumbents even when the incumbent lost. Incumbent losses are included because it is interesting to note the times when incumbents can be defeated. It would be better to have included all serious candidates in the data set, especially for elections in which there is no incumbent, but data on losing candidates is very difficult to obtain. We are, therefore, working with a hybrid data set, all winners and incumbent losers. The number of incumbent losers is small enough to make this a reasonable approach for many purposes.

TABLE 4
Percentages by which Gubernatorial
Candidates Outrun Their Party

Term	All	Conservative	Middle-of-the-Road	Progressive
1	5.5	2.6	15.8	4.8
2	16.1	12.5	36.2	11.7
3	13.8	7.4	37.0	22.1
4	15.2	10.8	25.1	24.3
5	8.0	7.3	13.7	4.2
6	9.6	11.4		0.3
7	- 2.8	- 2.8		

Note: The N's are the same as in Table 3. The level of party support is measured by the percentage of the party vote gained by either the conservatives or the progressives in the most recent House of Councillors election preceding the gubernatorial election. When the elections were held in the same year, the House of Councillors election is used no matter which came first. The denominator is the party vote, excluding votes for independents and minor parties. The numerator is either the vote for all conservative parties if the candidate is a conservative, or for all progressive parties if the candidate is either a progressive or a middle-of-the-road candidate. The parties classified as progressive are the JSP, JCP, Democratic Socialist Party, and Clean Government Party. Detailed data on the parties supporting a candidate were seldom available, so this approximation was used; it does a great deal of injustice to many candidates, particularly the middle-of-the-road candidates.

TABLE 5
Distribution of Non-Competitive Elections

Term	All		Conservatives		Middle-of-the-Road		Progressives	
1	8.3%	(112)	11.1%	(81)	5.3%	(19)	0.0%	(12)
2	41.6	(113)	37.4	(91)	76.9	(13)	33.3	(9)
3	36.9	(65)	32.7	(49)	66.7	(9)	28.6	(7)
4	40.7	(32)	37.5	(24)	50.0	(6)	50.0	(2)
5	31.6	(19)	28.6	(14)	66.7	(3)	0.0	(2)
6	28.6	(7)	33.3	(6)			0.0	(1)
7	0.0	(2)	0.0	(2)				

Note: Figures in parentheses are the N's from which the percentages were calculated.

While it is always advisable to bet on the incumbent in a Japanese gubernatorial election, the odds one should be prepared to offer vary depending on how many terms the incumbent has served. Japanese political commentators call this pattern the "second-term barrier": an incumbent is nearly invincible after his first term, but opposition gathers strength during his second term and the third election he contests is likely to be difficult. The existence of this "second-term barrier" can be demonstrated in several ways by looking at the "All" columns in Tables 2 - 5:

1. Although incumbents usually win, their success rate is lowest when running for a third term, excluding the small-N case of the sixth term. (Table 2)

2. The percentage of the vote going to the incumbent is highest in his second election and drops off sharply after the second term is completed. (Table 3)

3. Similarly, incumbents outrun their normal party vote by the largest margin in their second election. (Table 4)[11]

4. Noncompetitive elections are commonest after the incumbent's first term. (Table 5)

It might appear that the first three points are largely explained by the fourth—more noncompetitive elections—but as Figure 1 shows, the second-term barrier appears even when only competitive elections are examined. It also shows up in vote percentages in noncompetitive elections, with the protest vote (to a Communist candidate, say) at its lowest in the second election.

We should also examine the possibility that the second-term barrier pattern observed here might be characteristic only of conservative incumbents, since they are such a large proportion of the total. Looking again at

---

11. The national constituency elections to the House of Councillors was chosen to represent the level of conservative or progressive support in the prefecture because these elections are the most free from local influences and disturbances caused by variations in the number of candidates run by each of the parties. Election to the more important Lower House is by multi-member district, so a party may run multiple candidates or none at all. Only in the national constituency of the Upper House can one be sure the voters can choose among all parties.

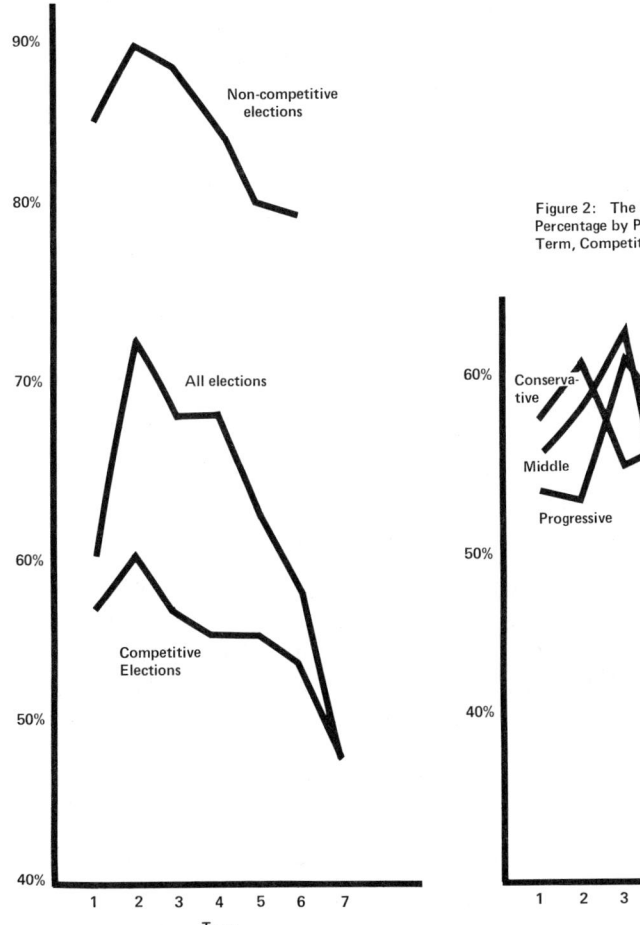

Figure 1: The Governor's Winning Percentage by Term and Competitive and Non-competitive Elections

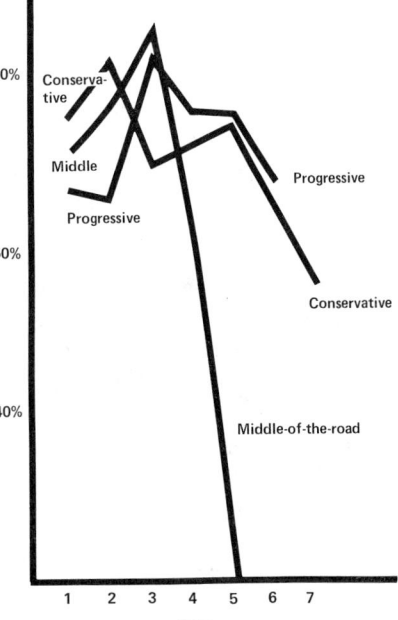

Figure 2: The Governor's Winning Percentage by Party Support and Term, Competitive Elections Only

Tables 2 - 5, we find that this is indeed the case: support for middle-of-the-road incumbents does not tail off notably after the second election, and progressive incumbents appear to grow in strength through their first three elections (the N's are too small to generalize thereafter). Figure 2, which excludes noncompetitive elections, shows a somewhat different pattern, but reinforces the point that the second-term barrier is a conservative phenomenon. In contrast to conservative candidates, who gain in strength in their second elections and fall off sharply in their third, the middle-of-the-road incumbents gain in both their second and third elections, while the progressives actually lose strength after their first term (if the conservatives oppose them at all), and then gain support during their second term in office. This is because a progressive is likely to be elected in the first place only when the conservatives are in some disarray. During his first term in office, either the conservative opposition remains fractionalized, in which case they put up no candidate at all, or it reunifies and fights a tough race. If conservative disunity was a factor in the first election, the conservatives have ample reason to unify against the progressive incumbent. It is also harder for the LDP, as the largest party in all prefectures and the clear majority party in most, to decide not to field a serious candidate. Progressives can expect competitive elections throughout their careers.

If the second-term barrier pattern explains the electoral record of conservative incumbents through the third election, what happens afterward? The conventional wisdom is that the alternating pattern will continue: having failed to dislodge the incumbent after two terms, the opposition loses heart (or the incumbent builds his strength anew) for the fourth election, but tries harder in the fifth. Tables 2 - 5 and Figure 2 demonstrate that this alternating pattern does indeed seem to be characteristic of conservative incumbents, and accordingly, of all governors in somewhat attenuated form.

We have succeeded in establishing the "normal" pattern: that incumbents usually win, but that for conservatives their strength is at its peak after their first term, and thereafter falls off in an alternating pattern. We can now get a better sense of how things work by examining some deviant cases. In particular, we may ask whether discontinuities in this pattern were caused by the rise of progressive strength in the late sixties and early seventies.

First, when were incumbents defeated after only one term, normally their strongest election? As Table 2 indicates, seven incumbents were defeated running for a second term. Six of these defeats may be attributed to the confusion surrounding the formation of the LDP in 1955. The merger of the Liberal and the Democratic Parties made sense on the national level because the JSP was threatening to take advantage of conservative disunity. In most prefectures, however, the JSP was no threat and the Liberals and Democrats had been the primary contestants for power. The two parties had less reason to cooperate in the prefectures and often refused to cooperate even after the merger. Thus, four of the second-term defeats involved contests between conservative candidates in this period. One more was a defeat of a conservative incumbent by a progressive probably made possible by conservative disunity. The remaining case which fits this explanation was a defeat of a middle-of-the-road incumbent by the newly unified LDP. The timing and form of these deviant cases strongly suggest that the most important disruption of normal patterns occured because of the formation of the LDP, not because of variations in the strength of progressive candidates. We shall return to this point below.

Second, we would not normally expect a noncompetitive election when there is no incumbent, but, as Table 5 shows, there were 10 such deviant cases. Four of these elections occurred in 1955 under the newly unified LDP. If the factions in the LDP could agree on a candidate, he was unbeatable, and the opposition parties accepted that fact in these four prefectures. In at least two other cases, the lucky candidate had been the vice-governor, and we may hypothesize that these candidates managed to appear as legitimate successors to the governors, running almost as incumbents. One more case is an extraordinary set of circumstances in Shiga Prefecture. In 1954, an independent conservative candidate named Mori defeated the incumbent Liberal Party governor. In the next election, the newly formed LDP gave its nomination to the incumbent Mori, but he was defeated by an independent conservative named Taniguchi. The 1962 race was a rematch between these two men, but this time the incumbent Taniguchi got the LDP nomination and Mori ran as an independent. Taniguchi won his second term in a five-way race with only one-third of the vote. If the progressives had managed to unite behind a single candidate, they could have won. Finally, in 1966, both Mori and Taniguchi retired and the LDP managed to agree on a candidate named Nozaki, who won with 83 percent of the vote against a token JCP candidate. Unfortunately, I have no background data on Nozaki, but we may guess that he was an ex-bureaucrat and perhaps a vice-governor. This is an extreme case reflecting the confusion caused by the formation of the LDP, but it illustrates the problems experienced by many prefectures. The Shiga case, then, fits into the "formation of the LDP" pattern even though the noncompetitive first election occurred 11 years later. Thus, we can explain 7 of the 10 cases by reference to the formation of the LDP or the succession of a vice-governor.

Let us summarize the findings of this section. First, the advantages of incumbency are great. We should expect truly competitive elections only when no incumbent is running, or when the incumbent has been in office a very long time. In particular, one should not expect a progressive to have a real chance of winning except when no incumbent is running and in those few prefectures in which the voters are fairly evenly divided between the two camps. In other prefectures, the election of a progressive requires serious splits within the LDP, and is most likely in a three-way race. Even in a three-way race, however, the progressives must unite behind a single candidate. Therefore, we should not expect progressive candidates to win very often, though once elected we can expect them to continue in office for several terms, even if the original election was a fluke three-way race.

Second, the advantages of incumbency are greatest in the election for a second term. In general, we should expect first elections to be the closest, followed by third and following elections, with the second election being the easiest for the incumbent. This pattern applies mainly to conservatives. Middle-of-the-road governors have the greatest second-term advantage, and maintain or increase that advantage through the third term. Progressives have little or no advantage in the second term, but the power of incumbency increases through the third or fourth term.

Third, part but not all of the advantage of incumbency is due to the decisions of opposition parties not to oppose the incumbent. However, the power of incumbency and the second-term barrier are evident in both competitive and noncompetitive elections.

Finally, analysis of deviant cases, second-term defeats, and first-term noncompetitive elections indicates that the major disruptions of these basic patterns were caused by the confusion resulting from the merger of the Liberal and the Democratic Parties, not by changes in the strength of the progressive camp.

One more variable predicts the percentage of the vote gained by a governor: the number of candidates running. This variable affects the vote in a rather mechanical way: the more candidates running, the less any given candidate is likely to receive. We are now in a position to develop an overall equation to predict election results. Table 6 presents the results of a multiple regression. Overall, these variables explain 70 percent of the variance. The presence or absence of competition explains 66 percent of the variance by itself, followed by the number of candidates and the term of the governor, all of which are statistically significant. Party support, whether a candidate is conservative, progressive, or middle-of-the-road, fails to reach statistical significance. Party support does not even reach statistical significance when we look at competitive elections only. The lack of statistical significance is surprising given the different patterns found above, but is an artifact of the small number of cases for nonconservative governors. The regression program does not recognize the theoretical significance of these several cases. In any case, the regression equation supports the overall conclusions reached above, and we can be fairly happy with the percentage of variance explained.

TABLE 6
Predicting the Governor's Percentage of the Vote

Variable	Beta	
Competition	-.735*	Multiple R = .838
Candidates	-.188*	R-square = .703
Term	.070*	Adjusted
Party Support	.034	R-square = .698
Party Vote	-.032	Std. Error = 9.534

Note: * indicates statistical significance at the .05 level. "Competition" is coded 1 for competitive and 0 for noncompetitive. "Candidates" is the number of candidates running. "Term" is coded 1 for the first election, 2 for third or later elections, and 3 for second elections. "Party Support" is coded 1 for conservatives and 0 for other. A third dummy for middle-of-the-road candidates added absolutely nothing to the explanation. "Party Vote" is the vote for the preceding House of Councillors election, as explained in the note to Table 4.

Electoral Trends

With this background in nomination and election politics, we can now return to an analysis of trends over time. In this section we will discuss the waxing and waning of progressive strength and look for periods in which the parameters of electoral politics changed. When did the major disruptions of the patterns described above occur? When were the turning points? We want to look particularly at the elections of 1955 and immediately thereafter for changes wrought by the formation of the LDP, the elections of the late 1960s and early 1970s when the rise of the new generation of progressive governors gained so much attention, and finally ask whether the elections of 1979 signify a return to politics as usual.

TABLE 7
Number of Governors by Party Support

Year	Conservatives	Middle-of-the-Road	Progressives	Not Conservative	N
1947	16	0	3	3	19
1948	16	0	3	3	19
1949	18	0	3	3	21
1950	20	1	4	5	25
1951	29	5	4	9	38
1952	28	5	4	9	37
1953	28	5	4	9	37
1954	27	6	4	10	37
1955	25	9	4	13	38
1956	25	10	6	16	41
1957	24	11	6	17	41
1958	25	11	7	18	43
1959	31	10	4	14	45
1960	32	9	4	13	45
1961	32	9	4	13	45
1962	34	6	4	10	44
1963	33	6	4	10	43
1964	36	4	4	8	44
1965	36	4	4	8	44
1966	35	5	4	9	44
1967	34	7	3	10	44
1968	34	7	3	10	44
1969	35	7	2	9	44
1970	35	7	2	9	44
1971	34	6	3	9	43
1972	32	5	6	11	43
1973	34	4	6	10	44
1974	31	4	8	12	43
1975	29	5	9	14	43
1976	25	5	7	12	37
1977	21	5	6	11	32
1978	17	4	5	9	26
1979	12	5	4	9	21

Note: Okinawa and Tokyo Prefectures were excluded from the analysis, so an N of 45 indicates complete data. Okinawa was excluded because it has not been a Japanese prefecture throughout this period. Tokyo was excluded because of its special organizational structure and its status as the capital.

First, let us try to document the trends in progressive strength over time. Table 7 presents the number of governors by party support for each year, although missing data make this information hard to interpret. The rise of a new generation of progressives is dated from the late 1960s because the models for this generation, Governor Minobe of Tokyo and Mayor Asukata of Yokohama City, were elected then. However, the increase in the number of progressive governors began only in 1970, and their numbers have never been very impressive. The rise of progressives was important more because of where they were elected and what they did in office rather than because of their absolute numbers. Progressives won in the major urban areas, and included the mayors of six of the nine largest cities. Japanese commentators assumed that these cities and prefectures represented the future of the rest of the country. Progressive governors and mayors also received a great deal of good press for the policies they initiated.

We should also note a small peak for progressives and a large peak for middle-of-the-road governors in the 1955-1959 period. This trend has gone largely unnoticed and unstudied, as have the problems for conservatives caused by the formation of the LDP. If the merger had been successful in most prefectures, we should have expected a rise in the number of conservative governors, but that occurred much later and was apparently due to the success of LDP economic policies.

We can get a better perspective on these trends by looking at elections, rather than the distribution of incumbents. Table 8 presents this information. Governors serve four-year terms, but since elections may be called early, several prefectures have fallen out of synchronization with the quadriennial "unified local elections." The best way to present the data, then, is by the unified elections and the three-year interim periods. The progressives' greatest electoral successes occurred in the 1972-1974 interim period. The worst period for conservatives was the 1956-1958 period after the formation of the LDP. This period saw some progressive successes but it was the middle-of-the-road candidates who picked up most of the slack left by the relative decline of the conservatives. The 1979 elections saw less of a conservative resurgence than an increase in the number of successful middle-of-the-road candidates. The 1979 elections thus resemble the 1956-1958 elections. This period, incidentally, was followed by a conservative resurgence.

TABLE 8
Governors Elected by Year and Party Support

Year	Conservatives		Middle-of-the-Road		Progressives		N
1947-50	81.5%	(22)	3.7%	(1)	14.8%	(4)	27
1951	77.4	(24)	12.9	(4)	9.7	(3)	31
1952-54	66.7	(8)	25.0	(3)	8.3	(1)	12
1955	69.0	(20)	20.7	(6)	10.3	(3)	29
1956-58	50.0	(8)	31.3	(5)	18.8	(3)	16
1959	74.2	(23)	16.1	(5)	9.7	(3)	31
1960-62	81.3	(13)	6.3	(1)	12.5	(2)	16
1963	76.7	(23)	16.7	(5)	6.7	(2)	30
1964-66	83.3	(15)	11.1	(2)	5.6	(1)	18
1967	75.9	(22)	17.2	(5)	6.9	(2)	29
1968-70	87.5	(14)	12.5	(2)	0.0	(0)	16
1971	74.1	(20)	14.8	(4)	11.1	(3)	27
1972-74	61.9	(13)	14.3	(3)	23.8	(5)	21
1975	69.6	(16)	17.4	(4)	13.0	(3)	23
1979	61.1	(11)	27.8	(5)	11.1	(2)	18

Note: The numbers in parentheses are the respective N's.

TABLE 9
Governors Elected by Year and Party Support (Nonincumbents)

Year	Conservatives		Middle-of-the-Road		Progressives		N
1947-50	80.8%	(21)	3.8%	(1)	15.4%	(4)	26
1951	69.2	(9)	30.8	(4)	0.0	(0)	13
1952-54	75.0	(3)	25.0	(1)	0.0	(0)	4
1955	66.7	(8)	25.0	(3)	8.3	(1)	12
1956-58	60.0	(6)	20.0	(2)	20.0	(2)	10
1959	90.0	(9)	0.0	(0)	10.0	(1)	10
1960-62	100.0	(6)	0.0	(0)	0.0	(0)	6
1963	75.0	(3)	25.0	(1)	0.0	(0)	4
1964-66	85.8	(6)	14.2	(1)	0.0	(0)	7
1967	71.4	(5)	28.6	(2)	0.0	(0)	7
1968-70	100.0	(3)	0.0	(0)	0.0	(0)	3
1971	80.0	(4)	0.0	(0)	20.0	(1)	5
1972-74	50.0	(5)	0.0	(0)	50.0	(5)	10
1975	40.0	(2)	20.0	(1)	40.0	(2)	5
1979	50.0	(3)	50.0	(3)	0.0	(0)	6

Note: The numbers in parentheses are the respective N's.

Given the advantages of incumbency, the election of new governors (nonincumbents) is the more reliable indicator of electoral trends. This information is presented in Table 9. Though we are now working with small N's, the trends do stand out more clearly in this table. The 1972-1974 elections were a truly great success for progressives; they won half of the new seats. The conservatives were really most successful in the years 1959 through 1971 and least successful from 1972 through 1979. The progressives did poorly in 1979 but it was middle-of-the-road candidates who were most successful.

We have documented changes in the fortunes of the conservative and progressive camps, but we must also ask whether these changes occurred within the framework of the overall patterns of gubernatorial elections or represented disruptions of these patterns. The most comprehensive way to approach this question is by using the regression equation developed above. When the equation fails to predict electoral outcomes, that suggests that the parameters of gubernatorial elections were changing. In what periods does the equation predict well and in what periods does it predict poorly? Deviations from the regression prediction are presented in Table 10. Both the average deviations and the average absolute deviations, ignoring the sign, are presented. When these figures are high, there were many deviant elections in that period.

TABLE 10
Average Deviations from the Regession Equation

Year	N	Average Deviation	Average Absolute Deviation
1949-50	8	0.10	6.55
1951	36	3.08	8.94
1952-54	19	-5.35	11.44
1955	33	0.48	9.38
1956-58	18	-1.37	6.81
1959	32	-1.12	5.81
1960-62	17	0.51	5.87
1963	31	1.69	6.64
1964-66	16	0.82	4.86
1967	31	0.53	6.94
1968-70	19	-2.50	7.62
1971	27	0.56	5.62
1972-74	20	0.88	5.08
1975	23	1.42	6.46
1979	20	-3.35	7.94

We should note first that the equation predicts fairly well in all periods. The basic patterns of gubernatorial elections have not changed much in the postwar period. The most deviant elections occurred in the 1952-1954 period, the years leading up to the formation of the LDP. The period of change may extend from 1951 through 1955, but does not continue after 1955. The elections of 1979 did deviate from normal patterns, but not by as much as in the earlier period. The only other period which deviates from the predictions is 1968-1970, the beginning of the new progressive era. That the two early periods of deviant elections, 1952-1954 and 1968-1970, preceded changes in the strength of the two camps, supports the argument that 1979 marks an important turning point.

Although we can point to two periods of deviant elections which were followed by changes in the fortunes of conservatives and progressives, it is difficult to interpret precisely what these deviations from the regression equation are picking up. Deviant elections should mean changing parameters, so we might be able to clarify our interpretation by looking at trends in two of the most important parameters: the advantages of incumbency, and the frequency of competitive elections.

TABLE 11
Gubernatorial Elections by Incumbency

Year	Winning Incumbents		Losing Incumbents		Incumbent Success Ratio	No Incumbent		N
1949-50	25.0%	(2)	0.0%	(0)	100.0%	75.0%	(6)	8
1951	62.9	(22)	0.0	(0)	100.0	37.1	(13)	35
1952-54	66.7	(10)	26.7	(4)	71.4	6.7	(1)	15
1955	55.2	(16)	17.2	(5)	76.2	27.6	(8)	29
1956-58	37.5	(6)	12.5	(2)	75.0	50.0	(8)	16
1959	63.3	(19)	13.3	(4)	82.6	23.3	(7)	30
1960-62	62.5	(10)	6.3	(1)	90.9	31.3	(5)	16
1963	87.1	(27)	0.0	(0)	100.0	12.9	(4)	31
1964-66	62.5	(10)	6.3	(1)	90.9	31.3	(5)	16
1967	75.0	(21)	10.7	(3)	87.5	14.3	(4)	28
1968-70	77.8	(14)	5.6	(1)	93.3	16.7	(3)	18
1971	77.8	(21)	0.0	(0)	100.0	22.2	(6)	27
1972-74	52.6	(10)	10.5	(2)	83.3	36.8	(7)	19
1975	78.3	(18)	0.0	(0)	100.0	21.7	(5)	23
1979	61.1	(11)	11.1	(2)	84.6	27.8	(5)	18

Note: Numbers in parentheses are the absolute number of cases.

Table 11 presents the trends in incumbency over time. First, the number of elections in which no incumbent is running is an indicator of how much change is possible in a given year. There were a great many open seats in 1951 and very few in the 1952-1954 period, but the figure levels off thereafter. In terms of the number of losing incumbents and incumbent success ratios, the deviant years are clearly 1952 through 1958 or 1959, the period before and after the formation of the LDP. The 1972-1974 and 1979 elections were somewhat deviant, somewhat less favorable for incumbents, but they do not stand out very much. Most of the changes that occurred in these periods happened in elections in which no incumbent was running.

Table 12 presents the trends in competitive and noncompetitive elections. A third category, "runaway" elections, was added to distinguish formally competitive but actually noncompetitive elections. The number of runaway elections is high from 1949 through 1955, suggesting that the parties had yet to learn how the system would work. During this period, the power of incumbency and the second-term barrier were being discovered and tested. After 1955, runaway elections were mostly replaced by noncompetitive elections: the opposition stopped challenging strong incumbents, particularly incumbents backed by a unified LDP. Three other elections stand out, all three for a relatively low number of competitive elections and a relatively high number of noncompetitive elections: 1967, 1971, and 1979. The elections of 1967 and 1971 do not seem deviant in any other sense. The elections of 1979 display a relatively low incumbent success rate and a high number of noncompetitive elections, a difficult combination to interpret.

Only one clear conclusion emerges from this analysis: the elections surrounding the formation of the LDP were the most deviant from overall patterns. This period deserves closer study. Although there are indications of parameter changes surrounding the rise of progressives in the late 1960s and early 1970s, we would be wise to conclude that these changes occurred within the framework of the basic patterns of gubernatorial elections that we have seen above. Progressives were increasingly successful during this period, but they won elections by adjusting to these patterns, not by overturning them. The elections of 1979 also appear deviant, but do not seem to have overturned basic patterns. Let us look at these elections more closely.

The argument that the 1979 elections signaled a decline of the progressives is based, first, on the fact that the three most outstanding progressive local executives all retired and were replaced by conservatives. This argument is based on the assumption that prefectures that have elected one progressive governor are more likely to elect another. Actually, it would be wiser to predict that progressive governors will be succeeded by a conservative. The reason for this somewhat counterintuitive argument is that the likelihood of maintaining the progressive coalition drops after the election of a progressive governor. Progressive governors have difficulty maintaining their coalition while in office, as concrete issues that divide the parties must be decided one way or the other. Once the governor retires, the coalition falls apart. That is what happened in both Tokyo and Kyoto. Moreover, I have found no case of a progressive being succeeded by another progressive in my data, though alternation between progressives and middle-of-the-road governors has occurred.

TABLE 12
Competitive and Noncompetitive Elections

Year	Competitive		Runaway		Noncompetitive		N
1949-50	62.5%	(5)	25.0%	(2)	12.5%	(1)	8
1951	60.0	(21)	28.6	(10)	11.4	(4)	35
1952-54	53.3	(8)	20.0	(3)	26.7	(4)	15
1955	53.6	(15)	25.0	(7)	21.4	(6)	28
1956-58	75.0	(12)	6.3	(1)	18.8	(3)	16
1959	42.9	(12)	17.9	(5)	39.3	(11)	28
1960-62	68.8	(11)	6.3	(1)	25.0	(4)	16
1963	48.4	(15)	22.6	(7)	29.0	(9)	31
1964-66	40.0	(6)	13.3	(2)	46.7	(7)	15
1967	28.6	(8)	17.9	(5)	53.6	(15)	28
1968-70	50.0	(9)	5.6	(1)	44.4	(8)	18
1971	37.0	(10)	11.1	(3)	51.9	(14)	27
1972-74	66.7	(12)	16.7	(3)	16.7	(3)	18
1975	60.9	(14)	21.7	(5)	17.4	(4)	23
1979	33.3	(6)	16.7	(3)	50.0	(9)	18
Total	50.6%	(164)	17.9%	(58)	31.5%	(102)	324

Note: Numbers in parentheses are the absolute number of cases. Noncompetitive elections are defined as those in which there was no opposition candidate or in which the only opposition came from Communist or minor parties. If two major party candidates ran, the election is not considered noncompetitive no matter what percentage of the vote that candidate received. In the early postwar years there are cases of a Socialist candidate looking much like a token. A runaway election is defined as a competitive one, but one in which the winner got more than twice the votes of any opposition candidate. These are formally competitive but actually noncompetitive. All other elections are considered truly competitive. Note that this definition of "competitive" does not necessarily mean that the race was a close one.

The more dramatic case of an incumbent progressive defeat, which occurred in Osaka in 1979, still fits this pattern. Governor Kuroda was opposed by a candidate supported by the LDP, JSP, DSP, CGP, and the New Liberal Club. Only the JCP continued to support the incumbent. Even so, he received 48 percent of the vote, making it a close race despite lopsided party support. In Iwate, an incumbent middle-of-the-road candidate, supported in his first election by the LDP and DSP, wound up with only the DSP backing him for a second term and was defeated by the LDP in a close three-way race. These two defeats represent extreme cases of progressives failing to maintain their coalitions. Where a coalition was maintained, as in Kagawa, the progressives won. In Kanagawa and Shinmane, incumbent progressive governors expanded their coalitions to include the LDP and, of course, won handily. A middle-of-the-road governor in Fukui was also reelected, with only token opposition from the JCP. In Akita, an ex-MOHA bureaucrat won with the support of the LDP, DSP, CGP, and the New Liberal Club against separate JSP and JCP candidates.

Progressives thus failed to succeed themselves, but they maintained most of their incumbents. However, they did fail to win any new seats. In three prefectures, Hokkaido, Ishikawa, and Fukuoka, joint JSP-JCP candidates failed to unseat multiple-term, and therefore presumably vulnerable, conservative incumbents. In Hokkaido and Fukuoka the incumbents had the support of the DSP and the New Liberal Club, which significantly lessened the progressive challengers' chances. None of these three elections should have been surprising. The elections of 1979 may have been slightly deviant in the aggregate, but I see no reason to expect that in 1979, or in the future, a progressive candidate with unified progressive support would have less chance of winning than at any other time in the postwar period. The key to progressive successes has always been cooperation among the progressive parties.

Some things did change in 1979. Within the normal patterns of elections, the number of progressive governors has declined. That is a significant fact in itself. Perhaps more significantly, the leaders of the progressives have left the scene, with no successors to the "star" role on the horizon. Finally, there is one factor which may strongly affect the chances of more progressive governors in the future: some progressive parties, notably the DSP, have moved toward supporting conservative governors. If the DSP or CGP has made a decision to move toward the right, perhaps in anticipation of a possible coalition with the LDP on the national level, the chances of obtaining progressive unity behind a single candidate may be lessened substantially. More broadly, at the moment there appear to be no more issues that are likely to bring together the progressive parties with good candidates from outside the parties. If the successes of progressive governors in the 1970s were due to such issues, their disappearance may herald a return to politics as usual. The differences, however, are in party strategy, not in basic electoral patterns, which have remained essentially unchanged in the postwar period.

Conclusions

We have covered a great many topics in this paper, and we should stop to summarize the major findings. First, gubernatorial candidates tend to be outsiders to prefectural politics and are more likely to be outsiders the more competitive the prefecture's politics become. Second, we demonstrated the great power of incumbency and the second-term barrier phenomenon. Third, we demonstrated that these patterns have not changed much over time. Fourth, we discovered that the greatest disruption of these patterns occurred in the period surrounding the formation of the LDP. Finally, we have suggested that the major variable determining the electoral fortunes of progressives and conservatives is the pattern of alliances among parties, and that these patterns may be changing.

More research could be done in this area. The period surrounding the formation of the LDP deserves more attention. A more thorough examination of nomination politics could be accomplished with more background data. The patterns of electoral politics could probably be clarified with more complete data, including background data and data on serious but unsuccessful candidates. Much more could be done in analyzing coalition patterns and the success of particular patterns over time. Thus, this paper only begins the process of understanding gubernatorial elections in Japan.

References

Chiba Nippo. April 4, 1975.

Chiba Prefecture Citizens' Movement Liaison Council. 1975. Chiba-ken no kankyō hakai to jumin undō (Citizens' movements and the destruction of Chiba prefecture's environment). The Chiba Prefecture Local Government Problems Research Center.

Kaminogō Toshiaki. 1978. Naimushō no fukkatsu (The rebirth of the Home Ministry). Bungei Shunju, March special issue.

Kim, Young C. 1968. Gubernatorial elections in Japan. Asian Survey, August.

Kyoto Prefectural Administration Study Group (ed.). 1973. Kyōtō minshū fusei (Kyoto's democratic administration). Kyoto: Yubonsha.

MacDougall, Terry. 1976. Japanese urban local politics: Toward a viable progressive party opposition. In Lewis Austin (ed.), Japan: The paradox of progress. New Haven: Yale University Press.

McKean, Margaret. 1977. Pollution and policy making. In T.J. Pempel, ed., Policymaking in contemporary Japan. Ithaca, N.Y.: Cornell University Press.

Nihon keizai shimbun. 1979. a. March 16. b. April 9. c. April 10.

Ohara Mitsunori and Yokoyama Keiji. 1965. Sangyō shakai to seiji katei: Keiyo kōgyō chitai (Industrial society and the political process: The Keiyo industrial region). Tokyo: Nihon Hyoronsha.

Reed, Steven R. 1980. Local policy making in a unitary state: The case of Japanese prefectures. Unpublished Ph.D. dissertation, Department of Political Science, University of Michigan.

Steiner, Kurt. 1965. Local government in Japan. Stanford: Stanford University Press.

Takaki Shōsaku. 1974. Chiji kōsen to chūō tōsei (The election of governors and central control). In Taniuchi et al.(eds.), Gendai gyōsei to kanryōsei (Modern administration and the bureaucratic system). Tokyo: Tokyo Daigaku Shuppankai.

Takayose Shōzō. 1975. Chihō jichi no saihakken (The rediscovery of local autonomy). Tokyo: Keiso Shobo.

Tsurutani, Taketsugu. 1977. Political change in Japan. New York: David McKay.

Tokyo University Social Science Group. 1965. Keiyo chitai ni okeru kōgyōka to toshika (Industrialization and urbanization in the Keiyo region). Tokyo: Tokyo Daigaku Shuppankai.

Toyama Shirō. 1975. Kakushin chiji (Progressive governors). Tokyo: Kokushō Books.

Zenkoku Shuchō Meibō. 1975. Tokyo: Chihō Jichi Sōgō Kenkyūjo.

Notes on Contributors

Soo Young AUH received a doctoral degree in political science at the University of Michigan. He is currently a research professor at the Institute of Foreign Affairs and National Security, Ministry of Foreign Affairs, Seoul, Korea.

John Creighton CAMPBELL is an associate professor of political science at the University of Michigan. He is the author of Contemporary Japanese Budget Politics and is currently working on a book about the government and the elderly in Japan.

Steven R. REED is an assistant professor of political science at the University of Alabama. His major research interest is intergovernmental politics and policy making.

Thomas R. ROCHON received his Ph.D. in political science from the University of Michigan in 1980 and is currently an Assistant Professor in the Department of Politics at Princeton University. He has written on aspects of Brazilian and Dutch political behavior and is presently working on studies of the French Socialist Party and of mass attachment to political parties in industrial democracies.

John STRATE is completing work on his dissertation in political science at the University of Michigan. He is currently a research associate at the National Aging Policy Center on Income Maintenance at Brandeis University and is doing research on private pensions. Other interests include the politics of industrial societies and social biology.

Minoru YANAGIHASHI is assistant professor of oriental studies at the University of Arizona. He has an M.A. from the University of California, Berkeley, and a Ph.D. from the University of Michigan. He is the author of several articles on Japanese foreign policy and relations, including contributions to Japan's Foreign Policy-Making (Hiroshi Itoh, editor) and to the Encyclopedia of Japan.

Jung-Suk YOUN is associate professor of political science at Chung-Ang University, Seoul, Korea, where since May 1980 he has been Dean of Student Affairs. He received an M.A. degree in Japanese Studies and a Ph.D. degree in political science from the University of Michigan. He was an undergraduate at Seoul National University.

MICHIGAN PAPERS IN JAPANESE STUDIES

No. 1. Political Leadership in Contemporary Japan, edited by Terry MacDougall.

No. 2. Politics, Candidates, and Voters in Japan: Six Quantitative Studies, edited by John Creighton Campbell.

No. 3. The Japanese Automotive Industry: Model and Challenge for the Future?, edited by Robert E. Cole.

No. 4. Survey of Japanese Collections in the United States, 1979-1980, by Naomi Fukuda.